101 Cheerleading Drills

Pam Headridge
Robb Webb

©2015 Coaches Choice. All rights reserved. Printed in the United States.

No part of this book may be reproduced, stored in a retrieval system, or transmitted, in any form or by any means, electronic, mechanical, photocopying, recording, or otherwise, without the prior permission of Coaches Choice. Throughout this book, the masculine shall be deemed to include the feminine and vice versa.

ISBN: 978-1-60679-315-2
Library of Congress Control Number: 2014946562
Cover design: Cheery Sugabo
Book layout: Cheery Sugabo
Text drawings: Robb Webb
Text photos (unless otherwise noted): Pam Headridge
Front cover photo: Pam Headridge

Coaches Choice
P.O. Box 1828
Monterey, CA 93942
www.coacheschoice.com

Dedication

To Pam's daughter, Misty: Thank you for asking me to be your cheer coach. Little did I know then that it would grow into a long, successful career!

To Pam's friend and fellow coach, Robin Gohn: It was a great ride!

To Pam's husband, Bill: You are my rock!

To Robb's nieces, Jasmin, Destiny, Cassie, and Kyah: Your smiles warm the world.

To Robb's friends, Lori Starnes Ward, Monica Martin, and Jodie Kanipe: I would like to express my gratitude for giving me a place to expand my knowledge of cheerleading.

To Robb's friend, Christy Glover: Thank you for helping me tap into my confidence.

To Robb's wife, Jenna: You are my driving force and inspiration.

Acknowledgments

We would like to thank Robin Gohn, Lauren Albritton, Crista Carlson, and the Oak Harbor High School cheerleaders for their help and support in this project.

Contents

Dedication	3
Acknowledgments	4
Introduction	6
Chapter 1: Jump Drills	9
Stretching Drills	
Static Stretching Drills	
Dynamic Stretching Drills	
Partner-Assisted Stretching Drills	
Strengthening Drills	
Functional Strengthening Drills	
Plyometrics Strengthening Drills	
Technique Repetition Drills	
Chapter 2: Tumbling Drills	49
Technique Drills	
Strengthening Drills	
Flexibility Drills	
Chapter 3: Motion Drills	83
Timing and Technique Drills	
Chapter 4: Stunt Drills	104
Trust Drills	
Strengthening Drills	
Resistance Band Drills	
Dumbbell Drills	
Medicine Ball Drills	
Technique and Timing Drills	
Top Person/Flyer Technique Drills	
Basing and Spotting Drills	
Stunt Group Drills	
Flexibility Drills	
About the Authors	176

Introduction

Cheerleading has exploded in numbers over the past two decades. No longer is it just girls on the sideline cheering their teams on to victory. Cheerleading has become a physically challenging sport. Running focuses on endurance. Wrestling emphasizes strength. Gymnastics demands balance, timing, and range of motion. Soccer depends on teamwork. A successful cheerleading team requires all of these physical and mental traits at both the individual and team level.

Building a successful cheerleading team requires development of a diverse mixture of physical and mental traits. Training starts by preparing a comprehensive individual and team conditioning program before the season begins. A sport-specific conditioning plan designed for cheerleading allows the development of proper technique and a higher fitness level plus decreasing the chances of injury. General development of strength, flexibility, endurance, speed, and basic building techniques are emphasized during the preseason period. Skills are maintained and strengthened by integrating coordinated team conditioning into daily training throughout the season.

101 Cheerleading Drills provides drills for a balanced plan to initially condition your new team and then sustain it throughout the season. Cheerleaders can increase their performance and maximize their skill level with a good conditioning program. These drills are directed toward individuals, small groups, and the team as a whole. Many of the drills involve two or more participants to facilitate team bonding and assist in the workout process.

The chapters are divided into jump drills, tumbling drills, motions drills, and stunting drills. Within each chapter, the drills are subdivided into exercises for stretching and flexibility, strength training and working proper technique. This organization allows you to find appropriate drills to facilitate the team's and individual's needs throughout the season. Each drill suggests a typical number of sets and repetitions per set to provide a general guideline, but how you allocate these drills depends on your cheerleader's weaknesses and strengths and is for you, the coach, to decide for the cheerleader. Treat the drills as building blocks, perfecting each progression before moving on to the next level.

During pre-season and early weeks, you should be choosing drills across the categories to emphasize the individual basics: endurance, strength, balance, speed, and range of motion. These should also be chosen to engage the full range of anatomy: upper and lower body kinetic and dynamic strength. More than any other sport (other than perhaps gymnastics), cheerleading requires engagement of the core strength and proprioception systems, which are critical for body control and balance. The brain integrates information from proprioception system into its overall sense of body positions, movements, and accelerations, which are fundamental to cheerleading. Build the core early and often.

Further into the season, your team begins to build choreographed routines/cheers, which integrate stunts, tumbling, jumps, and motions as elements. Team coordination is key. When the timing is off, when the stunts come down, when the jumps look weak, analyze the failures, drop back, and pick drills from the appropriate categories to rebuild momentum.

This book is intended for athletes, parents, and coaches. Throughout the book, the information is directed and written toward coaches, but will be very helpful to athletes and their parents. Knowledge of exercise principles, progression drills, and proper technique develops a safer and more effective program.

As with any conditioning program, an athlete must be in good physical shape to participate. All athletes should have a physical examination by a qualified doctor before taking part in cheerleading.

Protecting your cheerleader also means understanding your duties as the coach. You must provide a safe, physical environment with proper equipment to reduce risk and prevent injury. Supervise all activities closely. Accidents happen in cheerleading even with a well-planned conditioning program. Develop a written emergency plan of action, and be able to implement it. Educate your cheerleaders on the proper procedures when an emergency occurs. Have an emergency kit on hand at all times. Coaches need to have certifications in CPR/first-aid, concussion safety, and stunting progressions and techniques. The coach should also know the governing rules for cheerleading in their school, district, state, club, and/or program.

As cheerleading has evolved over the past several decades, so can your cheerleading program with this book. *101 Cheerleading Drills* is full of strengthening, stretching, and sport-specific drills. From jumps to stunting, your cheerleaders will improve; their toe-touches will get higher, and their motions and stunts will get tighter.

1

Jump Drills

Jumps exhibit energy, excitement, and athleticism, making them the quintessential part of cheerleading. Cheerleaders execute different types of jumps on the sidelines, in performances and during cheerleading competition routines. Well-timed, cleanly executed and sky-high jumps are one of the elements that define and highlight a team's athletic skill. Types of jumps include:

- Toe touch (Figure 1-1): The proper form at the top of the toe touch is the arms in a T-position slightly behind the legs; legs lifted up and out to the side as the hips rotate upward, knees turned toward the back, toes pointed, and torso lifted. A common misconception is that the hands touch the feet or toes. In reality, the arms stay in a T-position as the legs V-up and pass the arms. The back is always straight with the head up.

Figure 1-1. Toe touch

- Hurdler (Figure 1-2): A hurdler can be executed on either the right or left leg; however, it is good practice to drill both sides equally. Arms are extended straight out in a T, one leg is extended directly to the side or higher, knee locked, and toes pointed. The other leg is bent at the knee and elevated to the side in a hurdler position.

Figure 1-2. Hurdler

- Herkie (Figure 1-3): A herkie (named after Lawrence R. Herkimer, founder of National Cheerleaders Association) is basically the same jump as a hurdler with the exception of the arm placement. A herkie has one arm bent at the elbow with the hand on the hip, while the opposite arm is lifted straight up beside the head, often referred to as a touchdown position.

Figure 1-3. Herkie

- Front hurdler (Figure 1-4): This type of jump can be done on either the right or left leg. Facing diagonally, the cheerleader's arms are straight up beside the head as one of the legs is kicked out straight to the front and the other one is lifted back and bent with the knee pointing down toward the ground. Toes are pointed. The cheerleader should practice jumps on both sides to make the athlete more versatile.

Figure 1-4. Front hurdler

- Star or spread eagle (Figure 1-5): With a star or spread eagle jump, the cheerleader's arms hit a high-V pose, and the legs hit a reverse V position. The knees point to the front, and the toes are pointed.

Figure 1-5. Star or spread eagle

- Pike (Figure 1-6): For a pike jump, the cheerleader faces at a 90-degree angle to the audience. The arms and legs are extended straight out and are parallel to the floor.

Figure 1-6. Pike

- Double nine (Figure 1-7): At the top of the jump, the cheerleader's legs and arms form the shape of a 9, and are parallel to each other.

Figure 1-7. Double nine

In order for a cheerleader to perform an explosive jump, the process must be broken down into four steps: the approach, the lift, the execution, and the landing. The approach is the arm swing that generates the upward movement. The cheerleader uses strong, tight arm movements during the swing to assist in the propulsion off the floor. The lift is the explosive upward power achieved from the legs and arms as she propels herself off the floor. Leg strength is the driving force in this step. The execution is the skill demonstrated at the top of the jump. This step is where the different types of jumps are performed. Flexibility aids in demonstrating the proper technique in the skill as well as strong, tight movements. The landing is the return position to the floor. Often, cheerleaders fall out of the execution at the top of the jump and lose the precision of the landing. Teach the cheerleaders that all four steps are imperative for well-performed jumps.

An often-asked question by cheer coaches is: "How can I help my cheerleaders execute hyper-extended jumps?" The three key components are stretching, strengthening, and repetition through practicing. Stretching exercises enhance a cheerleader's level of flexibility. Strengthening drills increase vertical jumping ability. Repetition develops the proper timing and technique of jumps.

STRETCHING DRILLS

Stretching boosts a cheerleader's level of flexibility by increasing the joint's range of motion. Flexibility improves a cheerleader's performance because it takes less energy by the muscles around the joint to move through a greater range of motion. Muscle elasticity helps to prevent injury and soreness. Stretching also improves muscular balance and relaxation, increases the blood flow and supply of nutrients to the joints and surrounding tissues, and promotes improved performance and coordination.

Recommended stretching techniques for cheerleaders are static, dynamic, and Proprioceptive Neuromuscular Facilitation (PNF). Static stretching slowly puts the muscle into a position of controlled maximal or near-maximal stretch through elongation of the muscles and holding a certain position for a significant period of time, usually 30 to 60 seconds. Dynamic stretching involves moving parts of the body and gradually increasing scope and speed of movement. Proprioceptive Neuromuscular Facilitation (PNF) technique uses a partner in assisting the stretch. It is also called "contract-relax" technique.

The number of sets for each drill is dependent on the different stretching drills performed on a given day. If only executing a few key stretches, increase the number of sets for each drill to three to five sets. If doing a wide variety of stretches, one to two sets would be adequate.

Static Stretching Drills

Static stretching involves lengthening the muscle to its fullest and holding the position for an extended period of time. This method has been proven as a great means of enhancing flexibility. Other advantages to static stretching include:
- Easy to learn
- Requires little use of energy
- Allows adequate time to reset the sensitivity of the stretch reflex
- Helps to lengthen the muscle

#1: Seated Stretch

Objective: To develop optimal flexibility in the legs through static stretching, which, in turn, helps in the extension and form of jumps

Equipment Needed: Flat surface

Description:
- The cheerleader sits on the ground and extends her left leg sideways.
- The cheerleader bends the opposite leg with foot flat on the ground and the knee pointing upward.
- The cheerleader grabs the right ankle with the right hand and the left ankle with her left hand then lowers her upper torso toward her extended left leg and holds for 30 seconds.
- Have the cheerleader reverse legs and do the stretch on the opposite side for 30 seconds.
- Athletes should perform three sets.

Coaching Points:
- Monitor the cheerleader to assure that she holds the stretched position for 30 seconds with no release of tension. Often, cheerleaders relax during the process or fidget, causing them to not get the full benefit of this drill.
- If the cheerleader does not hold the position with pressure on the elongated muscle, she will not gain the needed elasticity in the inner thighs.

#2: Wall Split

Objective: To develop elasticity through the inner thighs using static stretching in order to perform hyper-extended toe touches

Equipment Needed: Wall surface, non-skid floor

Description:
- The cheerleader stands approximately three feet from the wall, facing away from the wall.
- Next, the cheerleader bends forward from the hips and places her hands on the floor for support.
- The cheerleader extends one leg behind her and against the wall.
- Slowly, the cheerleader slides her leg upward on the wall, using her hands on the floor to push her body against the wall, until she hits a split position.
- The cheerleader holds this position for 30 seconds.
- The cheerleader reverses legs and repeats the process.
- The cheerleader performs three sets.

Coaching Points:
- Form is an essential part of this drill. Check that the cheerleader's shoulders and hips are squared and the legs are straight. Do not let the cheerleader sacrifice proper technique in order to get her hips to the wall in a split position.
- Often, a cheerleader will not be able to hit a split in the beginning and needs to work toward this goal. Developing flexibility is a slow process and, if rushed, can cause injury.
- Stretching drills are a daily necessity to develop flexibility needed for jumps.
- This drill is also applicable for flyers in order for them to be able to perform heel stretches in stunts.

#3: Adductor Chair Reach

Objective: To develop range of motion in the inner thighs and lower back using static stretching

Equipment Needed: Non-skid surface, a chair

Description:
- While standing with her right side toward the chair, the cheerleader places her right foot on the seat, bending the leg at the knee.
- Keeping her left leg straight, the cheerleader leans forward at the hips and lowers her hands to the floor.
- The cheerleader will feel the stretch in her inside right thigh.
- The cheerleader must hold this position for 30 seconds.
- The cheerleader repeats this drill with the opposite leg.
- Have cheerleader execute three sets.

Coaching Points:
- The body weight needs to be evenly centered between the two legs as the cheerleader actively reaches toward the floor.
- Once she bends as close to the floor as possible, the position must be held for a minimum of 30 seconds with no bouncing.
- Do not let the cheerleader bend her support leg on the floor. Form is key to the success of this drill.

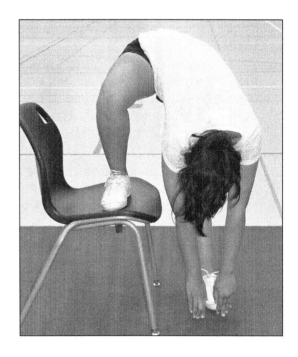

#4: Calf Stretch

Objective: To elongates both the calves, Achilles tendon, and the tissue behind the knees that, in turn, helps to prevent injury and muscle pulls

Equipment Needed: Even surface, a wall

Description:
- The cheerleader faces the wall and leans forward, placing her hands and elbows on the wall.
- The cheerleader extends her left leg straight behind her body with her heel raised as she bends her right knee.
- Slowly, the cheerleader shifts her weight forward as she presses her rear heel to the floor.
- The cheerleader holds this position for 30 seconds.
- The cheerleader reverses this skill for the opposite leg.
- After cheerleader masters this stretch, have her increase the hold to one minute per leg.

Coaching Points:
- Stretching through the calves relieves tightness and reduces the risk of leg and foot problems like plantar fasciitis, ankle strain, and shin splints.
- To stretch through the soleus (the muscle that starts just below the knee), bend the knee of the back leg to isolate and focus on this muscle and not the gastrocnemius.

Dynamic Stretching Drills

Dynamic stretching directly relates to the specificity of the stretching process as it links to the activity of jumping. In these stretches, the concentration is on the movements associated with jumping. Part of the challenge of jumping is getting the quick snap in the legs on the return phase of the jump. Dynamic stretching develops the ability to lift the legs up as high as possible and then to snap the feet down and together on the landing, all in a matter of a few seconds.

#5: Wall Kick

Objective: To develop explosive power needed in the legs for high jumps through dynamic stretching

Equipment Needed: Wall, non-slip surface

Description:

Wall Kick Version One
- Position the cheerleader to stand perpendicular to the wall with one hand touching it for support and balance. The other arm extends out from the body in a T-motion. The feet are together, and the back is straight.
- Using an eight-count sequence, the cheerleader takes four counts to slowly lift the leg as high as possible diagonally to the side, and then quickly snaps the leg back down on count five. She holds the start position for counts six, seven, and eight.
- The cheerleader continues the sequence for five sets, then she switches to the opposite leg, performing the same exercise for five sets.

Wall Kick Version Two
- On count one, the cheerleader quickly kicks the leg up diagonally to the side and as high as possible.
- The cheerleader slowly lowers it to the ground on counts two, three, four, five.
- The cheerleader holds the beginning position and relaxes on counts six, seven, eight.
- The cheerleader repeats the sequence for five sets, then switches to the opposite leg, performing the same exercise.

Coaching Points:
- The cheerleader must not bend forward or lean sideways at the waist when she lifts her leg. Check that her torso is up and her core is tight.
- This technique helps the cheerleader to practice the same lifted, straight-body form that is used while jumping. This means that the toes must be pointed and the supporting leg is straight.
- Keeping proper form and a lower leg lift is better than a high kick with the body out of alignment and legs bent. Do not let the cheerleader sacrifice form to get more height in the leg.

#6: Standing Kick

Objective: To develop range of motion in the hip joint through dynamic stretching; to reinforce proper form in jumps

Equipment Needed: None

Description:
- The cheerleader starts with her arms in a T-position and feet together.
- The cheerleader contracts her arms and squeezes her fists.
- Keeping the torso straight, hips and shoulders square, and chest up, the cheerleader kicks the right leg straight up and down 10 times while hopping on the opposite leg.
- The cheerleader repeats sequence on her left leg.
- The cheerleader does three sets.

Coaching Points:
- Often, the cheerleader wants to lean sideways toward the kicking leg. Stress that the body must stay in alignment from the head to the toes.
- Check to see that the cheerleader's kicking leg remains locked and toes pointed.
- Taking a photo of the cheerleader as she kicks will help her to understand how she is executing the movement and where she needs to correct her form.

Variation:
- The cheerleader kicks the right leg forward and to the right in a circle. This will start a clockwise rotation. She continues the rotation with the fullest range of motion possible until the foot has returned to its original place.
- The left leg performs a kick rotation to the right going clockwise.
- The cheerleader repeats the process with the left leg, going counterclockwise.
- The cheerleader repeats the sequence with the right leg, moving counterclockwise.
- These four reps require both legs to do a clockwise and a counterclockwise rotation. The cheerleader performs the four reps five times.

#7: Sitting Toe Touch

Objective: To work balance; to perfect proper toe touch form; to develop inner thigh muscles, working range of motion with dynamic stretching; to strengthen core muscles

Equipment Needed: Matted surface

Description:
- The cheerleader starts sitting on the floor with her knees and arms tucked into the chest. The feet are slightly off the floor and the back is rounded.
- Next, the cheerleader quickly extends the arms out to a T-position as the legs widen out to a toe touch pose.
- Then, the cheerleader pulls her legs back to the original position.
- Have the cheerleader do this drill 10 times, rest, and repeat two more sets.

Coaching Points:
- By stretching and strengthening these muscles, the legs gain the ability to extend up and out during the jumping process for a higher, wider toe touch.
- Have the cheerleader focus on good technique, keeping her toes pointed, her legs straight, and her back upright when hitting the toe-touch pose.
- In addition to the increased strength, this exercise helps the cheerleader to practice the proper technique of "sitting back" in her toe-touch jump.
- Do not let the cheerleader perform this drill on a hard surface because it will develop soreness and possible bruising around the tailbone.

Partner-Assisted Stretching Drills

Another way to lengthen muscles is through Proprioceptive Neuromuscular Facilitation (PNF). This method is a more successful way to develop range of motion than conventional stretching. It is a combination of an assist from outside source (a partner) and contraction of the muscle groups as the muscle is being stretched. PNF is thought to help reset the stretch reflex level or alter stretch perception according to a study done in 1996 by Magnusson, et al.* feet down and together on the landing, all in a matter of a few seconds.

Stock Foundry/Design Pics/Valueline/Thinkstock

*Magnusson, S.P., E.B. Simonsen, P. Aagaard, P. Dyhre-Poulsen, M.P. McHugh, and M. Kjaer. 1996. Mechanical and physiological responses to stretching with and without preisometric contraction in human skeletal muscle. *Archives of Physical Medicine and Rehabilitation*, 77(4):373–378.

#8: Partner Hamstring Stretch

Objective: To increase the flexibility in the hamstrings using PNF stretching

Equipment Needed: Flat, matted surface

Description:
- One cheerleader lies on the floor on her back with one leg extended in the air. The second leg is straight out on the floor.
- A partner stands on the floor facing the cheerleader and places her hands on the foot or calf of the leg that is extended in the air and applies gentle pressure backward on the leg.
- The cheerleader on the floor contracts the hamstrings isometrically and holds that position for a count of 15.
- They relax for 15 seconds and repeat the drill again, but this time the cheerleader on the floor does not contract the muscle as the partner actively and slowly stretches the leg. Hold this stretch for 30 seconds.
- The cheerleader repeats the drill for the other leg.
- The cheerleader performs one set.
- The cheerleaders switch places and repeat the drill.

Coaching Points:
- A concern about PNF stretching is a greater risk of injury if done improperly. Monitor the cheerleaders so they do not push too hard when assisting in the stretching process.
- Encourage the partners to communicate with each other in order to know the limit of the assist.
- If the cheerleader feels pain, immediately stop the stretch.

#9: Partner-Assisted Split

Objective: To develop flexibility in the legs; to enable the cheerleader to execute hyper-extended jumps with less risk of injury

Equipment Needed: Wall

Description:
- This drill takes two cheerleaders.
- Facing a wall, a cheerleader stands with one foot on the floor and lifts her other leg behind her, keeping it straight.
- The cheerleader places her hands and elbows on the wall for balance and support.
- The cheerleader's partner, standing behind her, sets the raised thigh onto her own shoulder. Interlocking her fingers, she positions her hands on the other cheerleader's buttocks.
- Using her shoulder, the partner carefully extends the thigh up while the other cheerleader contracts her leg and buttock muscles.
- The girls hold this position for 15 seconds. They relax for 15 seconds, then repeat the exercise, this time for 30 seconds.
- During this timeframe, have the partner apply gentle pressure upward on the leg.
- The cheerleader repeats the procedure on the other leg.
- The cheerleader performs one set.
- The cheerleaders switch places and repeat the drill.

Coaching Points:
- Often, a cheerleader is more flexible on one leg compared to the other. It is important to stretch both legs evenly to balance out the muscle groups.
- Educate your cheerleaders that flexibility has to be developed over time. Do not let cheerleaders use the excuse of "I am not flexible on my left leg" as a reason to not have proper technique on their jumps.
- This stretch is also good for flyers to increase their range of motion when doing arabesques and scales in stunting.

Variation:
- To balance out the legs muscles, the cheerleader should also stretch the back of the legs using the same approach except she will face away from the wall, extending her leg in front of her.

STRENGTHENING DRILLS

Cheerleaders use their leg muscles to explode off the floor in order to get enough height to execute the different body positions at the top of their jumps. Leg strengthening drills increase the vertical jumping ability and develop strong core muscles to help lift the legs into the air.

A variety of strengthening drills are important in your training regimen for three key reasons:
- The body tends to plateau when doing the same exercises because it becomes accustomed to the routine and adapts. Adding variety stimulates the muscle groups and causes the muscles to progress and aids in making bigger gains.
- Boredom is a key problem for athletes and, therefore, causes them not to work as hard as needed to progress in their sport. Varying drills keeps things fresh and athletes motivated.
- Each strengthening drill works the muscles from different angles and achieves different benefits. By adding variety, you can target and strengthen all needed muscles in order for athletes to execute great jumps.

Following are several drills that strengthen the key parts of the body for jumping.

Functional Strengthening Drills

Cheerleaders need to learn basic strength training exercises with proper technique and form before advancing to progressive drills that add complex movement. Starting with simple body-weight moves, the cheerleader executes few repetitions/sets until the movement is mastered, then increasing the number and degree of difficulty. Strength training not only works the muscle groups, making them stronger, but also incorporates balance and stability throughout the body.

#10: Stationary Squats

Objective: To work the quadriceps and hamstrings, developing strong legs for vertical lift

Equipment Needed: Non-skid surface

Description:
- The cheerleader starts with the feet shoulder-width apart, slightly turned out, and arms extended out in front of the body. The chest is up, the back slightly arched, and the core section tight.
- The cheerleader slowly lowers into the squats, concentrating on placing the body weight into the heels, keeping the knees over the toes and arms straight out in front and parallel to the floor. She must not lean forward. The goal is to have the hips back as if sitting in a chair. The cheerleader must not let the knees move forward.
- On the ascent to the beginning position, the cheerleader drives the hips up and forward.
- The cheerleader starts with only two sets of 10 repetitions and work up to five sets.

Coaching Points:
- Squats are the benchmark of high-quality lower torso training. Bottom line: form is more important than how low a cheerleader can bend.
- Teach body weight squats where the thighs (femur or thighbone) are parallel to the floor, sitting back into the position and minimizing the range of motion at the ankle and maximizing the range of motion of the knee.
- This drill is also great drill for bases to do to develop stronger legs for stunting.

Variations:
- Once the athlete can properly perform these body weight squats, add lightweights or a medicine ball to the hands.
- Once the proper squat form is mastered, the cheerleader bends her knees and as she straightens her legs, she kicks her right leg out to the side, then places it back to shoulder-width from the left leg as she returns to the bent-knee position. She then straightens her legs again and kicks her left leg out to the side, and then squats again bringing her leg foot back to the ground.

#11: Split Squat

Objective: To enhance single-leg strength and dynamic flexibility in the hip flexor muscles

Equipment Needed: Non-skid surface

Description:
- The starting position begins with the cheerleader's right leg in front of her body.
- The cheerleader keeps the front knee over the ankle and lowers the back knee to the floor.
- The cheerleader centers the body weight between the two legs, keeping the back up tall, head erect, and the hands behind the head.
- The cheerleader looks straight ahead.
- The cheerleader slowly lowers the back knee toward the ground until the front thigh is parallel to the floor. Her body, from the head to the knee, should follow a straight line to the floor.
- The cheerleader returns to starting position by straightening her legs.
- The cheerleader repeats this process five times, and then switches legs and repeats five more sets.

Coaching Points:
- This exercise is not a lunge because the feet are stationary.
- To prevent injury, the knee must align over the ankle.
- Once mastered, add the twisting action of the torso as the cheerleader lowers her back knee to the floor. This move increases the range of motion of the hip flexors.

Variation:
- The cheerleader holds a medicine ball in front of her chest with her elbows bent to her side.
- The cheerleader repeats the same procedure as listed in description.
- As the cheerleader lunges, she reaches to one side of the leg with the ball and leans toward the ground.
- The cheerleader returns to starting position and brings the ball back to her chest.
- The cheerleader repeats the drill and reaches to the opposite side with the ball.
- The cheerleader switches to other leg and repeats.

Variation

#12: Calf Raises

Objective: To strengthen the gastrocnemius and soleus muscles

Equipment Needed: None

Description:
- The cheerleader stands with her feet shoulder-width apart.
- The cheerleader slowly lifts up on to the balls of her feet, and then presses the heels back down to the floor.
- The cheerleader repeats sequence 30 times.
- Have the cheerleaders rest, and then repeat five more sets of 30 reps.

Coaching Points:
- The muscles used in this drill help the cheerleader get height off the floor in order for her to perform the jump skill at the execution point.
- Emphasize to the cheerleader to squeeze the ankles together as she lifts upon her toes. In turn, this part will strengthen the ankles, too, and prevent the cheerleader from rolling her feet outward when landing her jumps.

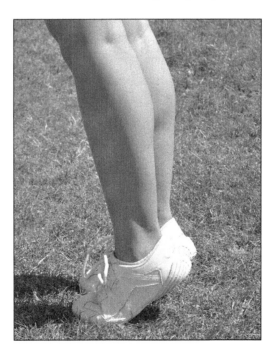

#13: Sit Lift

Objective: To work the core muscles which assist in both the lifting and snapping down of the legs when jumping

Equipment Needed: Matted surface

Description:
- The cheerleader lies on her back on a padded surface with arms extended overhead in a touchdown position and the legs together and extended straight.
- The cheerleader lifts her legs up, keeping them tightly together as her torso rises from the floor, forming a V-position or pike-up, at the height of the execution. Her arms are extended toward her legs.
- The cheerleader returns to the starting position with her back and legs on the floor.
- Repeat five times for one set. The cheerleader does five sets.

Coaching Points:
- Strengthening the core is key to all parts of cheerleading, but especially in the jump section. Often, cheerleaders tend to lean forward at the top of their jumps, causing poor form. With a strong core section, cheerleaders learn to lift upward from the midsection, keeping their back straight, in order to achieve the needed height.
- These drills are excellent body awareness drills, duplicating the leg positions the cheerleader hits at the top of her jumps.
- Once all three variations are mastered, have cheerleader perform a continuous combination of all the pike-up, straddle-up, and tuck-up. One combination equals a set. Cheerleader does five sets.

Variations:
- Straddle-Up Sit Lift
  - ✓ The cheerleader starts lying on the surface with legs extended, together, and straight. Arm is kept straight above the head.
  - ✓ In a quick motion, the cheerleader brings her legs upward and apart in a straddle. At the same time, her arms extend out toward her toes while she does a sit-up.
  - ✓ The cheerleader returns to the starting position.
  - ✓ Repeat five times for one set. The cheerleader does five sets.
- Tuck-Up Sit Lift
  - ✓ The cheerleader starts lying on the floor as in the other variations.
  - ✓ Next, while keeping her legs together, the cheerleader bends her knees to her chest as she lifts her legs and body upward. At the same time, her hands and arms reach past her knees while she executes a sit-up.
  - ✓ The cheerleader then returns to the starting position.
  - ✓ Repeat five times for one set. The cheerleader does five sets.

Variation—Straddle-Up Sit Lift

#14: Leg Toss

Objective: To strengthen the abdominal and back muscles

Equipment Needed: Matted surface

Description:
- This drill needs two people.
- One person lies on her back on the floor with her legs and arms extended.
- The second person stands, with her feet apart, by the head of the cheerleader lying on the ground.
- The cheerleader, on the floor, grabs the ankles of the standing person for stability. She lifts her legs, keeping them straight and together, up to her partner.
- The standing cheerleader tosses the lifted legs toward the ground as the floor person resists the downward movement.
- The standing cheerleader should randomly toss the legs forward and sideways.
- Cheerleaders repeat this drill 10 times, and then change positions and repeat.

Coaching Points:
- As the cheerleader's legs are tossed downward, check to see that she never lets her feet touch the ground in between the throws. This technique will force the cheerleader to contract her abdominals while resisting the tossing of her legs and strengthening the hips and core.
- The cheerleader on the floor should keep her legs tightly together and toes pointed to promote proper form.
- The cheerleader on the floor should not arch her back. Monitor to see that the back stays tight to the floor during the toss process.
- Do not let the cheerleader bend her knees during the entire drill.
- The standing cheerleader needs to throw the legs with some force in order for this drill to be effective.

#15: Hanging Leg Lifts

Objective: To work full range of motion of the abdominal and hip flexors in order to hit the leg positions at the top of the jumps

Equipment Needed: Secure overhead bar suspended from the wall, ceiling, or two poles

Description:
- The cheerleader suspends himself from an overhead bar with straight arms.
- The cheerleader lifts his legs upward and outward in a straddle movement as high as possible, contracting through the hip flexors and abdominal muscles.
- The cheerleader returns his legs down and together toward the floor.
- The cheerleader repeats this drill five times.

Coaching Points:
- This exercise is difficult to execute in the beginning, so perseverance is needed. Start off with the cheerleader hanging from the bar with no leg movement for 5 to 10 seconds to develop the arm strength needed to perform the drill.
- Next step, encourage the athlete to lift the legs straight out in front as high as possible for two times. The cheerleader may only be able to lift the legs slightly off the floor. Recognize the small successes so the cheerleader will eventually gain enough strength in the midsection, enabling him to perform the drill as described.

Variations:
- At the top of the lift, the cheerleader can also demonstrate the following leg positions in place of the straddle lift: hurdler, pike, star.

Variation—pike

Variation—hurdler

Plyometrics Strengthening Drills

The following strengthing drills use an explosive method called plyometrics. This technique enhances the quick reaction of the cheerleader through powerful muscular contractions as a result of rapid eccentric contractions. This method develops swift and powerful jumping. These movement drills performed in training match the movement encountered in performance and competition. Focusing on the development of the leg muscles will help the cheerleader to achieve the height needed to execute the skill at the top of the jumps. Emphasize speed and power rather than endurance. Direct careful attention to technique used during the exercise.

#16: Tuck Jump

Objective: To develop powerful quadriceps

Equipment Needed: None

Description:
- The cheerleader starts with feet together and hands at her side.
- The cheerleader claps her hands together overhead on count one, two.
- On count three, the cheerleader circles her arms down and across the body.
- The cheerleader bends her kness on count three.
- On count four, the cheerleader hits a T-position with her arms as she tucks her kness to her chest.
- The cheerleader circles her arms back down on count five as her feet return to the floor, and she immediately bends in order to spring up into the air and performs another tucked position jump with arms in a T-position on count six.
- The cheerleader bends her knees again, circling her arms on count seven and propels off the floor on count eight as she again tucks her knees and hits a T-position with her arms.
- The cheerleader rests for a count of eight.
- The cheerleader repeats this drill 10 times.

Coaching Points:

- Have the cheerleaders perform all jumps to counts for both timing and perfection. Assigning counts synchronizes everyone's understanding of where and when to execute each part of the jump, causing everyone to perform the jumps together.
- The cheerleader must keep the torso lifted on the tuck jumps. Leaning forward stops the upward momentum.
- A tuck jump is an excellent example of plyometrics triggering the legs to explode off the floor.
- Landing is key to proper technique. The athlete must learn to land on the balls of the feet, then push the heels to the ground in order for the muscles to absorb the downward movement.
- Toes should be pointed forward while landing in order to prevent rolling the ankles.

#17: Pencil Jump

Objective: To strengthen the legs; to teach proper technique; to synchronize the cheerleaders' approaches to the jumps

Equipment Needed: None

Description:
- Cheerleaders start with feet together and arms at their sides.
- On count one, all cheerleaders clasp their hands together.
- On count two, they hold clasp position.
- On count three, their arms extend over their heads with hands still together. Their feet remain together.
- On count four, they hold overhead clasp position.
- On count five, they circle their arms down and cross their body, releasing the clasp and bending their knees.
- On count six, they jump off the floor with arms in a T-position and legs together and straight.
- On count seven, they land on the ground with knees bent and arms at the side.
- On count eight, they stand with legs straight.
- They repeat sequence 10 times.

Coaching Points:
- Explain the difference to your cheerleaders betweeen a clap and a clasp. For a clap, a cheerleader brings her palms together with fingers straight. In contrast, for a clasp, the cheerleader brings the palms together and the hands fold over each other, squeezing the palms tightly.
- Check to make sure everyone is jumping the same height off the floor as they hit a strong T-position.
- Head and eyes should always be up. Often, cheerleaders tend to look down at their feet when jumping.

#18: Hops Across the Floor

Objective: To develop explosive leg power

Equipment Needed: None

Description:
- Starting position is feet together and arms in a touchdown position. Several cheerleaders can execute this drill at the same time.
- With feet and legs together, cheerleaders hop across the gym until they reach the other side.
- The cheerleaders return back to their starting position, hopping on one foot across the gym.
- They repeat hopping across the floor on the opposite foot and return to their original position hopping on both feet.

Coaching Points:
- This is also a great areobic workout for the cheerleaders.
- Make this more enjoyable by playing fun, upbeat music in the background. Also using fast-paced music will set the tempo and speed of the jumping.
- Add another element of fun by dividing the group into teams and challenging them to see which team can complete the task the quickest.

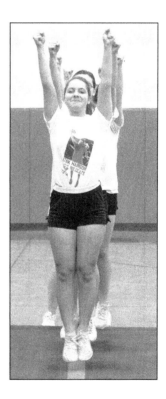

#19: Frog Squats

Objective: To strengthen the quadriceps, hamstrings, glutes, and calves in order to increase their vertical lift in jumps

Equipment Needed: Flat surface

Description:
- The cheerleader starts with feet apart. Her back remains straight.
- The cheerleader squats low and touches the floor with her fingertips.
- The cheerleader jumps upward and clicks her legs together at the top of the jump. At the same time, her arms extend above her head, reaching as high as possible.
- The cheerleader returns her feet to the ground in a squat with her feet apart and her fingers touching the floor.
- The cheerleader keeps her head up and abdominals contracted throughout sequence.
- The cheerleader performs the drill five times.

Coaching Points:
- Watch that the cheerleader does not bend from the waist in order to touch the floor. A deep squat is needed in order to get low enough. The thighs should be parallel to the floor. For some cheerleaders, this deep squat will take time to master.
- During the squat position, the cheerleader must have her knees positioned directly over her toes. Do not let her roll the hips forward.
- Squats are functional exercises that improve both the upper and lower body strength as well as promote mobility and balance.

#20: Agility Box

Objective: To strenghen the ankles; to develop speed, power, and agility in the legs

Equipment Needed: Area marked off in a five dot dice pattern on the floor (This can be done by placing small "X" marks with tape or paint dots on the floor.)

Description:
- The basic concept is to have the student jump in patterns from one dot to another.
- The cheerleader starts at the edge of the pattern.
- With both feet together, the cheerleader jumps to the bottom right corner dot, then to the bottom left corner dot with only one foot.
- Next she jumps to the center dot with both feet, then to the top left corner dot with one foot, and on to the top right corner dot with both feet.
- Next, the cheerleader jumps backward, repeating the pattern of alternating jumping from both feet to one foot.
- This is one set. The cheerleader repeats the pattern five times.
- The patterns can be done entirely on one foot, as well.

Coaching Points:
- Have the cheerleader start slow to perfect the sequence. Gradually increase the speed as her technique improves.
- This drill requires maximum effort in order for it to improve speed and agility. Technique, energy, and speed need to work together for greatest benefit.
- The cheerleader needs to absorb the impact of the jump through the entire foot.
- Once pattern is mastered, time the cheerleader as she performs the required sequence five times through as fast as she can. Her goal is to improve her time.
- The benefit of this exercise is to move the feet and hips fast, using proper body control. Because all movement begins off the floor, the cheerleader learns how to apply force into the floor and propel her body in the needed direction quickly.
- This quick agility skill can be appled to not only jumps but tumbling, dance, and motions.

Variation 1:
- With both feet, the cheerleader starts on the bottom right dot, hops around the outside dots.
- Next, the cheerleader hops backward around to the outside dots on both feet.
- The cheerleader repeats the drill on one leg.
- The cheerleader hops around the outside dots backward on one leg.

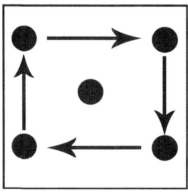

Variation 1

Variation 2:
- The cheerleader starts off the box with her feet together.
- The cheerleader hops with her feet apart, with her right foot on the right corner dot and her left foot on the left corner dot.
- Next, the cheerleader hops with her feet together to the center dot.
- Next, the cheerleader hops with her feet apart to the top corner dots; her right foot is on the right corner dot, and her left foot is on the top left corner dot.
- The cheerleader hops with her feet together and turns to her right as she lands with both feet on the center dot.
- The cheerleader jumps with both feet apart on the bottom corner dots.

Variation 3:
- The cheerleader starts off the box.
- The cheerleader hops on both feet onto the bottom right corner dot.
- Next, the cheerleader jumps to the bottom left corner dot.
- The cheerleader hops on both feet to the center dot.
- The cheerleader jumps on both feet to the top left corner dot.
- The cheerleader moves to the top right corner dot.
- The cheerleader hops back to the center dot.
- The cheerleader hops back to the bottom right corner dot.
- The cheerleader repeats the sequence on one leg.

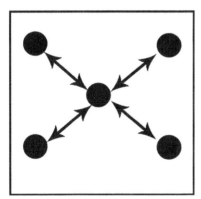

Variation 2

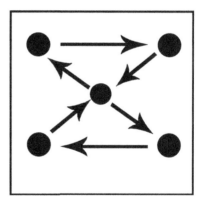

Variation 3

Technique Repetition Drills

Once the muscles are well-conditioned and the cheerleaders understand the proper technique to propel their body off the floor, practicing each type of jump daily will help to achieve explosive, super-high jumps. Repetition is the best way to develop strong legs and proper form. Following are several ways to run through jump training and prevent boredom and monotony.

#21: Jump Conditioning

Objective: To build stamina and endurance; to develop group timing

Equipment Needed: None

Description:
- Organize the cheerleaders into a window formation so the coach can see everyone. Play fast-paced music, and start counting in eight-counts as cheerleaders perform the following sequence:
    - ✓ Count one: Cheerleaders hit a high-V arm position with feet together.
    - ✓ Count two: They hold high-V position.
    - ✓ Count three: They bend their knees as they swing their arms downward in a circular position, crossing in front of their body.
    - ✓ Count four: They jump off the floor and hit the top of the jump.
    - ✓ Count five: They land the jump with feet together, knees bent, and arms at their sides.
    - ✓ Count six: They hold the landing position.
    - ✓ Count seven: They straighten legs to a standing position.
    - ✓ Count eight: The cheerleaders hold the standing pose.
- Using the count sequence, cheerleaders go through the following sets of jumps:
    - ✓ The cheerleaders do 10 repetitions of eight-counts, hitting a pencil jump on count four. This makes 10 sets of pencil jumps.
    - ✓ Next, they do 10 sets of eight-counts, performing tuck jumps on count four of every eight count.
    - ✓ Next, they do 10 sets of eight-counts executing left hurdlers jumps on count four.
    - ✓ Lastly, they do 10 sets of eight-counts demonstrating right hurdlers on count four.
    - ✓ Use four sets of eight-counts for a rest period.
    - ✓ Then, the cheerleaders repeat the sequence, executing 10 sets of pike jumps, 10 sets of toe touches, 10 sets of right front hurdlers, and 10 sets of left hurdlers. Repeat the four sets of eight-counts as a rest period.

Coaching Points:
- Depending on the tempo of the music, the cheerleaders will perform 80 jumps in an 8- to 10-minute timeframe.
- Tailor the routine to fit your squad's physical ability. Start off with fewer total number of jumps, and as the weeks progress, increase that number.

#22: Jump Lines

Objective: To perfect jump technique; to improve synchronization

Equipment Needed: None

Description:
- Depending on the number of cheerleaders, line them up with four to six athletes in each row. Play upbeat music, or count out loud in eights.
- The front row of cheerleaders performs a designated jump to one set of eight-counts.
- Next, they move to the back row, and the new row executes the same jump to one set of eight-counts.
- The cheerleaders repeat this pattern until each cheerleader moves through the rows and performs the same jump five times.
- Next, change to a new jump that the front line must demonstrate and continue rotating through the lines as before.

Coaching Points:
- Either buy a CD that has a person counting out loud from one to eight several times and at different tempos, or record your own count to a CD or mp3 player.
- Jump lines switch things up enough to add variety to keep the cheerleaders' interest and also help synchronize their timing.
- This drill helps the coach easily watch and evaluate the cheerleaders in the front row for proper technique.

Variation:
- To both increase their cardiovascular system and work jumps at the same time, have the cheerleaders in the back rows jog in place as the front row performs the designated jump.
- For variety, switch up the cardio part by substituting jumping jacks, knee lifts, marching, and arm swings in place of the jogging.

#23: Jump Circle

Objective: To perfect jump technique; to work timing

Equipment Needed: None

Description:
- Six to eight cheerleaders form a circle facing inward.
- Setting the jumps to eight counts, the cheerleaders perform their jumps at the same time.
- Monitor their sequence so that all the cheerleaders are moving the same, both timing and placement, from start to finish.

Coaching Points:
- By facing each other, they can watch their timing to make sure they are in sync.

Variation:
- Have each cheerleader in the circle perform the jump one at a time while the others critique her form.

#24: Pool Jumps

Objective: To train in an environment that provides greater resistance, thereby strengthening the muscles necessary to perform jumps

Equipment Needed: Pool, lake, or beach with chest deep water

Description:
- The cheerleader starts in chest-deep water with feet together and arms in a T-position.
- The cheerleader dips down and propels herself off the bottom of the pool into the air as she extends her legs out to a straddle position.
- The cheerleader lands with her feet together and back on the floor of the pool with knees slightly bent.
- Five repetitions equal one set. Have the cheerleader do five sets.

Coaching Points:
- The extra buoyancy allows the cheerleader to practice snapping her legs back together while adding the resistance from the water.
- Give this drill to the cheerleaders to practice during the summer off-season months.
- Performing jumps in a pool adds an element of fun to the exercise.

Variation:
- The cheerleader can perform different leg movements at the top of the jump in the water: pike, double nine, and hurdler.

2

Tumbling Drills

Tumbling is a vital part of cheerleading especially in the competitive arena. Being a good tumbler is a key element that often guarantees a person a spot on the cheerleading squad. Gymnastics skills are the hardest skills to teach and must be learned over time with proper progressions. Tumbling did not become a major part of cheerleading until organized competitions developed in the 1980s. Before that time, the primary tumbling elements were cartwheels and splits. Nowadays, cheerleaders perform advanced-level tricks like back handsprings, tucks, layouts, and full twists.

Too often, cheerleaders think they can learn to do a tumbling skill, like a standing back handspring, in a couple weeks. With no tumbling background, that desire is often not obtainable. Many basic skills must be mastered before a person can achieve a back handspring. Strength must be developed in the legs, back, abdominals, shoulders, and arms. Back flexibility is also a key factor. Cheerleaders must start with the basics and progress to the desired skill. Safety is always a primary concern. Never have them practice advanced tumbling without a knowledgeable coach and spotter plus a padded surface.

A spotter is a person who provides physical assistance during a tumbling skill. She will stand close to the tumbler and be prepared to move the cheerleader. A spotter must know where and when to place her hands during the skill and how much force to use. For most skills, the spotter places her hands near the tumbler's center of gravity, which is near her hips. A spotter's hands should be in place at the start or before the tumbler executes the skill.

Strength, power, speed, endurance, balance, agility, coordination, and proper technique are required in executing gymnastic skills.

TECHNIQUE DRILLS

Because a cheerleader throws her body weight in different directions as well as upside-down while tumbling, she needs to develop proper technique. In all the tumbling drills, the following procedures should be executed from the onset:

- Start with feet together.
- Maintain strong arm positions.
- Execute powerful takeoffs.
- Sustain a tight core.

Focusing on these four key factors helps the cheerleader to concentrate on proper form at all times, creates muscle memory, and aids in keeping tumbling safe. Have the cheerleaders practice the following drills to gain tumbling proficiency.

#25: Forward Roll

Objective: To develop body awareness and proper form

Equipment Needed: Matted surface, foam block

Description:
- The cheerleader stands with her feet together with the foam blocked squeezed between her ankles. Legs are straight and arms extended overhead. The elbows are tight to the head, and the whole body is vertically aligned.
- The cheerleader leans forward from the waist and reaches out to the floor. The head, shoulders, and arms move as one component.
- The cheerleader puts her hands on the floor as far forward as possible without jumping.
- The head stays in line with the arms, and the chin is tucked in as she begins the roll. The hips follow.
- The arms bend as the back slowly touches the floor.
- As the cheerleader completes the forward roll, her hands grasp the knees.
- As her feet hit the floor, the cheerleader pulls her body up to a standing position and adds a hop (rebound) to the end.
- The cheerleader must keep the foam block between her ankles throughout the process.

Coaching Points:
- When first learning to tumble, your cheerleaders need to master the proper technique of a forward roll.
- Often, cheerleaders learned this skill when they were young and have bad habits they need to correct due to improper form.
- Two key factors to a forward roll are: when first starting the process, the cheerleader reaches as far forward to the floor as she can, trying to bend her knees as little as possible, and secondly, to stand up out of the roll without the assist of her hands pushing her body off the floor.

#26: Tight Body Drill

Objective: To develop body awareness

Equipment Needed: Matted surface

Description:
- Two cheerleaders are needed for drill.
- One cheerleader lies on the floor on her back in a straight body position with her arms overhead.
- The partner grabs her feet and slowly lifts her body upward.
- The partner hold the cheerleader up for a count of five, then slowly lowers her back to the ground.
- The cheerleader on the floor must not bend at the knees, hips, or waist.
- The group repeats the pattern five times.
- The cheerleaders reverse positions and repeat the sequence.

Coaching Points:
- Often, cheerleaders have a hard time translating an idea into reality with their bodies. This drill is an easy, low-risk way to teach cheerleaders exactly what a tight core means and how to perfect the skill.
- A tight body with a strong core is needed not only in tumbling, but also when flying in a stunt.
- Every time a cheerleader becomes loose in the body, have them immediately perform this drill so they can physically grasp the concept again.

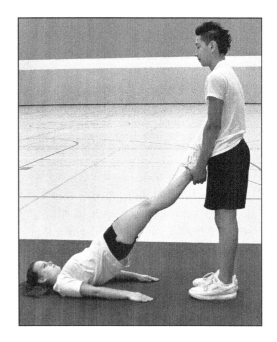

#27: Cartwheel

Objective: To develop body awareness, strong arms, and a tight core

Equipment Needed: Matted surface and masking tape; mask off a straight line on the mat or floor approximately 15 feet long

Description:
- The cheerleader starts at one end of the line, facing in, with her arms extended above her head.
- The cheerleader steps forward with her right leg as she reaches out to the floor, placing her right hand on the line followed by her left hand. The elbows are straight, and the core is tight.
- The left leg lifts off the floor, followed by the right stepping leg. The body is now upside-down. The legs are directly over the torso, opened in a V-position. Both hands are on the line, and the legs are fully extended.
- As the legs continue through the overhead rotation, the right foot lands on the line, followed by the left foot. The torso remains tight, and the arms follow and finish overhead.
- The cheerleader does five cartwheels.

Coaching Points:
- The cheerleader can start stepping forward with either her left or right leg.
- Chalk an outline of the cheerleader's hand placement on the floor so you can see judge the proper position and distance to reach.
- Mastering the correct technique of a cartwheel will help your cheerleaders progress to the more difficult tumbling skills. Perfection before progression is needed for both safety and understanding proper technique.
- Cartwheels are ideal tumbling moves to use when transitioning in the cheer motion and dance section of a routine. When done properly, they are very visual and easy to synchronize.

Variation:
- Once this drill is mastered, encourage your cheerleaders to perfect a one-arm cartwheel on the line and then progress to an aerial.

#28: Round-Off

Objective: To turn horizontal speed into vertical speed

Equipment Needed: Matted surface

Description:
- The cheerleader steps her left leg forward, bending her knee into a lunge position.
- Her arms are extended toward the ceiling and tight beside her ears.
- The cheerleader leans forward, twisting the hands and shoulders as her hands are placed on the floor.
- The first hand is twisted 90 degrees, and the second hand is about 180 degrees from the direction of travel.
- The cheerleader hits a handstand position, legs and feet together, facing the opposite direction from the way she started.
- The cheerleader snaps her hips down quickly and lifts her chest to create backward momentum.

Coaching Points:
- Round-offs can be done starting with either the left or right leg.
- The cheerleader must master a cartwheel before progressing to a round-off.
- Round-offs can also be done by running and hurdling into it.
- Draw hand outlines on the floor with chalk to guide the cheerleader in proper placement.
- Arms need to push away from the floor when hitting the landing.
- Both hands come off the floor at the same time when the cheerleader snaps her hips down and lifts the chest up during the landing.
- On the landing, the cheerleader does not pike the body.
- Add a rebound, a quick upward jump, after the landing. This will help the cheerleader lead into other skills from the round-off.

#29: Handstand

Objective: To build strength in the shoulders and arms; to develop overall balance

Equipment Needed: Matted surface

Description:
- The cheerleader stands with her arms extended straight above her head and tight to the ears.
- The cheerleader kicks up her right foot and takes a large step forward into a lunge.
- The cheerleader leans her entire body toward the floor, maintaining a straight line from the tip of the fingers through the trunk to the extended left leg.
- The hands should be placed on the floor a body-length away from the starting position.
- The legs and body swing up to a handstand position with the head in neutral position, looking at the hands. The supporting right leg lifts up to the left leg. The cheerleader maintains a vertical line from head to toe and does not hollow the back.
- When the weight is over the hands, the cheerleader needs to keep the force centered in the base of the hands for balance. She does not bend the elbows or knees.
- Have the cheerleader step back down, maintaining a vertical line with her body to the starting position.
- The cheerleader performs this drill 10 times.

Coaching Points:
- In the beginning, have spotters on both side of the cheerleader to catch the cheerleader's legs when she hits the handstand. This way, the cheerleader can focus on her technique without fear of falling.
- A second option is to have the cheerleader practice this drill against a wall. This will help with proper alignment. Do not let the cheerleader use the wall as a support crutch, but as a balance point.
- The cheerleader needs to have an appropriate lunge, not too short, in order to make it up onto her hands. Many novice tumblers tend to bend at the waist and reach too close to their feet instead of stretching out away from their starting position.

- Teach the cheerleader to control the lift into the handstand. If she puts too much power into the push-off from the legs, she could end up falling right through the handstand.
- Maintaining a straight body is key to hitting the handstand.
- Tell the cheerleader if she falls, to tuck her head to her chest so not to injure her neck.
- Once she can hold the handstand, challenge the cheerleader to perform a controlled half turn when she hits the handstand before stepping back to the floor.
- Once the handstand is mastered, she bridges over backward to the floor, or she rolls forward out of the handstand.
- Perfecting a handstand is important because most tumbling skills pass through a handstand position.
- Strong handstands will improve the cheerleaders' skills in both tumbling and stunting.

Variation—Handstand Pop:
- Using the same beginning technique as described in the handstand drill, the cheerleader lifts her body into a handstand.
- As she hits the top with the body in alignment, she quickly pops off her hands by shrugging her shoulders and snapping back to the original starting position. She should not hollow her back or bend her elbows and knees. For the blocking of the shoulders, the cheerleader needs to extend and engage her shoulders. The muscle tension gives her better control. To understand the blocking technique, have the athlete stand with her arms extended overhead. Ask her to lift or shrug her shoulders without bending her arms. She must squeeze her shoulders tight to her head at the same time.
- The cheerleader does several handstand pops across the gym floor and back.
- An easier option is to have the cheerleader stand, facing a wall. She extends her arms straight out toward the wall. She leans into the wall and shrugs her shoulders and maintains locked-out arms as her hands hit the wall. She pops off the wall, using only the shoulder shrug and a flick of her wrist.

Variation—Handstand Pop

#30: Handstand Forward Roll

Objective: To advance gymnastic skills by adding two tumbling elements together

Equipment Needed: Padded surface

Description:
- The cheerleader hits a handstand position with arms straight, body aligned over her shoulders, and head in a neutral position between her arms.
- The cheerleader bends her arms and tucks her chin in her chest. Her center of gravity starts to shift forward.
- The cheerleader rounds to her upper back and rolls out.
- The cheerleader pulls her body into a slight tuck position and rolls across her back.
- The cheerleader finishes the roll, plants her feet onto the floor, and stands up.

Coaching Points:
- Spotting by another person is required during the initial attempts at this skill.
- The cheerleader should not stick her head out from between her arms when rolling.
- The cheerleader should not arch her back, or else she will fall flat on her back and miss the rolling position.

#31: Bridge

Objective: To work back, shoulder, and wrist flexibility; to develop skills needed to execute front and back walkovers

Equipment Needed: Matted surface, extra mats

Description:
- The cheerleader begins standing with her feet shoulder-width apart and her arms extended overhead, tight to the ears.
- The head, arms and shoulders move as one unit.
- The cheerleader looks straightforward as she arches her back and reaches for the floor.
- The cheerleader does not bend her knees as she starts but pushes her hips forward.
- The cheerleader slowly leans back, reaching for the floor and placing her fingers as far away from her feet as possible. She keeps the arms and knees as straight as possible for as long as possible, remembering to push the hips forward in order to keep the center of gravity over her feet.
- Once her hands are on the floor, her fingertips will be facing her heels. The cheerleader does not lift her heels off the floor when her hands reach the ground.
- Her head should be tucked in between the shoulders and not looking at the floor.
- Once in the bridge position, the cheerleader straightens her arms and legs as much as possible and holds this position for 10 seconds.
- The cheerleader returns to the starting position by reversing the moves, or she can kick over her legs to a standing position.
- The cheerleader repeats the bridge five times.

Coaching Points:
- Many cheerleaders have a fear of going backward and want to look back and to the side as they start the backward movement, causing poor body alignment. To alleviate this fear, have spotters on both sides to prevent the cheerleader from falling on her head.
- An easier version to do a bridge is to add a layer of mats behind the cheerleader. Doing so enables her to not have to bend as far. She can concentrate more on proper body mechanics. As she perfects each step, remove a mat until no mats are left.

#32: Back Walkover

Objective: To develop the precursor to back handsprings; to increase back flexibility

Equipment Needed: Matted surface

Description:
- The cheerleader begins standing with her back to the mat and her arms extended overhead.
- The cheerleader arches backward and places her hands on the mat as she lifts one leg off the floor. The head, arms, and shoulders move as one unit.
- Her legs hit a split position as her body hits the handstand position.
- Her head stays in alignment with the shoulders and arms.
- The first leg continues out of the split to the floor, and the cheerleader walks out of the handstand by bring the other leg over the top to the floor.
- The cheerleader repeats this maneuver across the mat. Depending on the size of the mat, have the cheerleader perform at least 10 of these exercises.

Coaching Points:
- A cheerleader must have mastered both the handstand and bridge in order to perform this skill properly.
- Place spotters on both sides of the cheerleader when first learning the back walkover skill.
- Have the cheerleader perform the walkover slowly in order to develop proper technique and control.

#33: Hollow Position

Objective: To strengthen and perfect the hollow body position needed in many tumbling skills

Equipment Needed: Matted surface

Description:
- The cheerleader is on the floor in a push-up position.
- The cheerleader drives her hands into the floor, depresses her shoulders, and hollows her chest.
- At the same time, the cheerleader tucks her pelvis, squeezes her abdominals, locks out her arms, and tightens her legs.
- The cheerleader maintains the hollow position while lifting one leg off the floor.
- The cheerleader reverses the procedure and lifts the other leg.
- The cheerleader performs this sequence 10 times.

Coaching Points:
- Check to assure that the cheerleader maintains a straight body position throughout the drill. She should not pike at the waist and lift her derriere into the air.
- To add more difficulty, a training partner can test the cheerleader's body tightness by applying moderate pressure to her upper back and buttocks when in the hollow body prone position. The cheerleader must remain tight and stable. The training partner should exert light pressure on the cheerleader in the beginning. Once the cheerleader has mastered correct body position, the partner can increase the pressure on the upper back and buttocks.

#34: Sit Back

Objective: To learn the proper approach of a back handspring

Equipment Needed: Mats and a knowledgeable spotter

Description:
- The cheerleader starts with feet together, standing tall, and hands by her side.
- The spotter kneels to the side of the cheerleader with one knee on the floor and the other one bent to serve as a platform for the cheerleader to sit.
- The cheerleader claps on counts one, two.
- The cheerleader swings her arms down to her side on counts three, four.
- On count five, six, the cheerleader sits back on her partner's knee as she swings her arms up overhead. Her chest is up, and she pulls her hips back as though she is sitting in a chair. Her feet are flat on the floor. This is the position a cheerleader uses just before she executes a back handspring.
- The spotter reaches up and prevents the cheerleader from falling backward during the sit momentum.
- The cheerleader performs this drill five times.

Coaching Points:
- The natural tendency for the cheerleader during the sit phrase is to lean the chest forward. This is poor technique and will cause the cheerleader to jump up inappropriately during the next sequence of the back handspring, causing her to undercut the landing.
- Breaking down the parts and perfecting each step of a back handspring helps the cheerleader achieve her goal. Often, cheerleaders only think about the ending process in learning this skill and are unable to perform the back handspring properly and safely because they have not perfected the parts leading up to it. Do not let the cheerleader progress until she has mastered the sitting approach.

#35: Jump Back to Candlesticks

Objective: To develop strong muscles and proper technique in order to perform a back handspring

Equipment Needed: Foldable mats or multiple mats stacked two to three feet high

Description:
- The cheerleader stands with her back to the mat and her arms extended up by her head.
- The cheerleader swings her arms down as she sits back.
- Then as the cheerleader brings her arms in front of her and pushes hard off the floor with both feet, extending her legs and jumping back to the mat in a hollow body position.
- The cheerleader lands on the mat on her lower back with her arms extended and squeezed tightly to her head.
- The cheerleader pushes her hips upward as she pulls her legs toward the ceiling.
- The cheerleader hits a candlestick position with hips in the air.
- The cheerleader does this drill 10 times.

Coaching Points:
- Too often, cheerleaders tend to jump straight up when learning back handsprings. This drill teaches them to jump up and backward, elongating their takeoff.
- Breaking down the process into sections and perfecting each part will strengthen cheerleaders' execution and develop correct technique.
- When landing on the mat, the tumbler needs to land on her lower back not her butt. Landing on her lower back puts her in the proper position to use her hips to rotate in a back handspring.
- At the end of the drill, the tumbler should keep a tight, hollow position and not pike as she pushes her hips toward the ceiling.

#36: Jump Back to Partner

Objective: To learn proper takeoff technique for a back handspring

Equipment Needed: Mats

Description:
- A strong, knowledgeable spotter is needed to assist this drill.
- Start with a cheerleader standing on a matted surface with another cheerleader directly behind her.
- The front cheerleader swings her arms down to her side, then up over her head as she bends her knees and jumps up and backward.
- The second cheerleader or spotter, standing behind the cheerleader, catches the first cheerleader around the hips/waist area, lifts her up overhead, and then places the cheerleader back onto her feet. The spotter assists in the upward movement of the cheerleader, maintaining strong, tight arms.
- Have the cheerleaders repeat this drill five times.

Coaching Points:
- The cheerleader should push her hips upward to help generate rotation momentum and develop body awareness of the proper steps to a back handspring.
- The jumping cheerleader sustains a tight bodyline with her hips upward as she practices this drill. Too often, the cheerleader will relax when in the air, causing a problem on controlling the lift and direction of her body by the spotter. A relaxed body could cause the cheerleader to be dropped and possibly injured.
- The spotter needs to dip from the knees to catch the cheerleader at the top of the jump. It is absolutely necessary to keep her arms contracted and straight as she catches the cheerleader in order not to get hit in the face.

Variation:
- The front cheerleader swings her arms down to her side, then up over her head as she bends her knees and jumps up and backward; the same as in the description.
- The spotter, standing to the side of the cheerleader, catches the tumbler at the hips and thighs with her hands and tilts the cheerleader toward the floor. The spotter should stabilize herself with her feet apart and absorb the impact with her legs. She should be able to spot on both sides of the cheerleader to avoid overuse injuries.
- The tumbling cheerleader places her hands onto the floor, hollows out her body and the spotter then flips her over onto her feet.
- The tumbler keeps her arms close to her head and supports her own body weight as her feet are flipped to the floor.

Variation—starting position

Variation—the catch

Variation—the dismount

STRENGTHENING DRILLS

Strong muscles are necessary for the cheerleader to perform tumbling skills, to protect the joints, and to prevent injury. A cheerleader must be able to exert force (her body weight) against a resistance (the floor) as she tumbles. It takes a combination of strength and power. To gain these necessities, an overload principle must be utilized, and resistance must be progressively increased. More muscle power means the cheerleader places less strain on joints and connective tissue.

#37: Triceps Dip

Objective: To strengthen triceps and anterior deltoid

Equipment Needed: Chair

Description:
- With her back to the chair, the cheerleader places her hands on the front of the seat with the fingertips facing toward her body.
- The cheerleader slowly lowers her body toward the floor by bending her arms until there is a 90-degree angle between the upper arm and forearm.
- The cheerleader keeps her elbows close to her body.
- The cheerleader's weight is centered in her arms.
- The cheerleader straightens her arms, pushing against the chair, and returning herself back to the starting position.
- This sequence completes one rep.
- The cheerleader takes 15 seconds to complete this task.
- Athletes should perform 10 reps.

Coaching Points:
- Check to see if the chair is stable and can handle the athlete's body weight.
- The cheerleader needs to keep her shoulders down while bending her elbows during the dip.
- Have the cheerleader inhale as she lowers her body and exhale as she pushes her body back up.
- Strengthening the triceps and anterior deltoid will assist the cheerleader to punch-off the floor on handsprings.

Variation—Straight Legs:
- The cheerleader starts sitting on a mat with her legs extended straight out in front of her.
- The cheerleader places her hands with her elbows bent on a box that is behind her.
- The cheerleader straightens both her body and arms as she lifts her torso off the floor into a plank position.
- The cheerleader slowly bends her elbows as she lowers her body back to the floor.

Variation—Straight Legs

#38: Wall Sit

Objective: To strengthen the quadriceps muscles in order to gain power in tumbling passes

Equipment Needed: Wall, two- to five-pound weights

Description:
- The cheerleader stands with her back to the wall.
- The cheerleader hits a "sit" position with her back maintaining contact with the wall.
- Her heels are directly under her ankles and the knees are at a 90-degree angle.
- The cheerleader holds this position for a count of 30.
- The steps outlined to this point count as one rep.
- Athletes should perform three reps.

Coaching Points:
- Watch the cheerleader's form as she executes this exercise. Check to verify that her back maintains contact with the wall and she contracts her abdominal muscles. Her hips and shoulders are squared out.
- The cheerleader's body hits two right angles; one at the hip line against the wall and the other at the knees.
- Do not let a cheerleader do this drill if she has existing knee problems because much of the body weight is centered on the knees.

Variations:

- As she sits against the wall, the cheerleader extends her right leg straight out in front of her and holds that position for 30 seconds. She repeats the same move, extending her left leg.
- Place two- to five-pound weights in the cheerleader's hands. As she hits the sit-position, she extends her arms straight out in front of her. She holds this pose for 30 seconds.

Variation—with weights

#39: Wall Handstand Push-Ups

Objective: To strengthen the upper body; to teach the cheerleader to control her body in an inverted position

Equipment Needed: Wall, a folded mat or pillow

Description:
- The cheerleader faces the wall and places her hands on the floor.
- The cheerleader places a mat on the floor beneath the head.
- With her elbows straight, the cheerleader kicks her legs straight up into a handstand with her back against a wall.
- The cheerleader slowly bends her arms, lowering her head to the floor, and then straightens her arms, pushing her head off the floor and her body upward.
- The goal is to have the cheerleader be able to do five push-ups.

Coaching Points:
- Check to make sure that the cheerleader keeps her core tight. She should not pike at the waist or arch the back while holding the handstand position.
- If this drill is too challenging, start with the cheerleader holding a static handstand position against the wall for 30 seconds. Have her do this drill five times.
- Other exercises to master in order to progress to handstand push-ups is have the cheerleader hit a push-up position on the floor with the legs elevated on a box behind her.

#40: Serratus Punch

Objective: To stimulate the small muscle groups and promote stability in the shoulder joint

Equipment Needed: Two- to five-pound weight

Description:
- The cheerleader lies on the floor with her back tight to the ground and the legs bent.
- With weights in both hands, her arms are extended toward the ceiling with her fists facing toward each other.
- Using her shoulder muscles, the cheerleader pulls her arms toward the ceiling, keeping the elbows straight. She lifts her shoulders off the floor and then returns them back to the ground. She should feel like she is pinching her shoulder blades together.
- The cheerleader carries out 10 repetitions.
- The steps outlined count as one set.
- The cheerleader completes three sets.

Coaching Points:
- Because of the overhead movements done in tumbling and stunting, muscular strength is needed in the shoulders.
- The cheerleader starts with two-pound weights and does more repetitions. As the drill becomes easy, have the cheerleader increase the size of the weights.
- The weights can also be replaced with a medicine ball.

#41: Twisted Wrists

Objective: To strengthen the muscles in and around the wrist, fingers, and forearm

Equipment Needed: A two-pound weight, a three-foot piece of rope, and a two-foot stick or round bar (Tie the weight to one end of the rope, and fasten the other end of the rope to the center of the stick.)

Description:
- The cheerleader stands with her feet shoulder-width apart.
- The cheerleader grabs the stick on each end with her hands.
- The cheerleader holds the stick parallel to the floor with her elbows out.
- Slowly, the cheerleader twists the stick, rolling the string around it causing the weight to lift up off the floor. She continues this process until the weight reaches the stick.
- The cheerleader slowly reverses the twisting movement and lowers the weight back toward the floor.
- The cheerleader performs five sets.

Coaching Point:
- A clockwise rotation develops the wrist flexor, and a counterclockwise rotation works the wrist extensors. Working both sides of the wrists creates balance in the muscle groups.

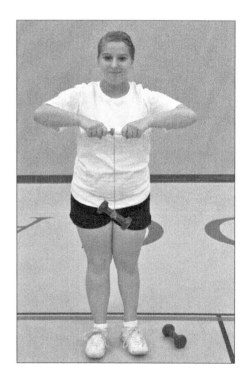

#42: Reverse Leg Lift

Objective: To build strength in the hamstring muscle group and the lower back

Equipment Needed: Mats

Description:
- The cheerleader lies face down on the mat with both her arms and legs extended straight out.
- As she inhales, the cheerleader lifts one leg, keeping it straight and toes pointed, as high as possible and holds for a count of five.
- Then, the cheerleader returns the leg back to the floor as she exhales.
- The cheerleader reverses to the other leg and repeats the exercise.
- The cheerleader performs five sets.

Coaching Points:
- The cheerleader must stabilize her body in order not to roll her hips laterally. Her hipbones stay on the floor, and the top of the foot must face the floor at the highest point of the lift.
- Hamstring strength is essential to balancing out overdeveloped quadriceps and assisting in injury prevention.
- To increase the range of motion in the legs, place two mats on the floor under the cheerleader's thigh area and have her extend her leg upward off the mats.

Variations:
- As the cheerleader raises one leg, she also lifts the opposite arm off the floor. She performs five sets.
- Have the cheerleader perform the same exercise with ankle weights.

#43: Lying Hamstring Curls

Objective: To develop strong gluts and hamstrings

Equipment Needed: Resistance bands

Description:
- Tie the two ends of a resistance band together to make a circle. The cheerleader lies on the floor on her stomach with her left leg straight out on the floor and the right leg bent at the knee and foot extended toward the ceiling.
- The cheerleader places the band around the instep of the left foot and around the right ankle.
- The cheerleader curls the right leg, bringing her heel toward her buttocks, without moving her right thigh off the floor. The left leg contracts keeping the toe of the foot and the left thigh on the floor.
- The cheerleader does 25 curls.
- The cheerleader reverses the band and curls the left leg toward the buttocks.

Coaching Points:
- Watch the cheerleader's hips and lower back. If they begin to move, the cheerleader has reached her limit of movement in her joints and must rest. If she contracts her abdominal muscles, this will help to prevent hyperextending the lower back.
- Moving the heel closer to the butt or increasing the resistance of the band increases the intensity of the movement.

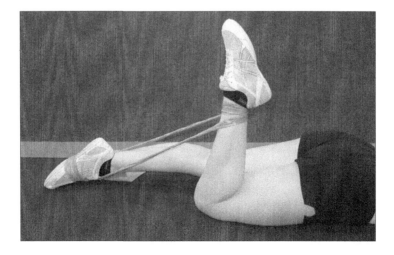

#44: Partner-Assisted Hamstring/Quad Curls

Objective: To develop strong gluts, hamstrings, and quadriceps

Equipment Needed: None

Description:
- One cheerleader lies face down on the floor with legs extended straight and arms flat on the floor and reaching over the head.
- The partner kneels on the floor by the cheerleader's feet.
- The cheerleader on the floor bends her right knee and lifts her lower leg off the floor toward her buttocks as her partner resists the upward lift by pulling against her ankles.
- The cheerleader returns her legs to the floor as her partner pushes against her ankle.
- The cheerleaders perform two sets of 10 repetitions and then switch roles and repeat.

Coaching Points:
- This drill develops muscles critical for fast flexion of the knee and extension of the hip during running tumbling.
- Monitor the floor cheerleader's hip for stability. Her upper thighs remain in contact with the floor. Check that she does not arch her back during the partner-resistance phrase. If her hips come off the floor, the partner is adding too much resistance and needs to ease back a bit.
- This drill works both the front and back of the legs, balancing out the muscle groups.

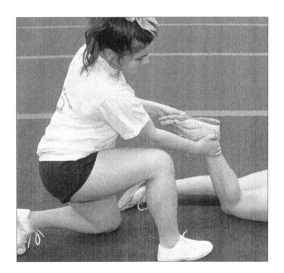

#45: Planks Series

Objective: To build overall strength and stability in the entire body from the neck to the shoulders and through the core into the back and legs

Equipment Needed: Matted surface

Description:
- The cheerleader starts in a push-up position on the floor. He performs this series for 10 seconds working up to 30 seconds.
- Following are two basic positions for this drill:
  - ✓ Basic plank: The hands, forearms, and toes support the body on the ground by placing the hands and forearm flat on the floor with the toes curled under the feet. The body is extended out parallel to the surface, tilting the pelvis, and pulling the belly button toward the spine, keeping the mid-section in alignment and allowing no sagging in the middle. The cheerleader is looking at the floor.
  - ✓ Side plank: Lying on his side, the cheerleader lifts himself up onto his left forearm and left side. He maintains a straight line from the top of his head through his body to the bottom of his feet.
- The steps to the sequence, using both the basic and side plank positions, are as follows:
  - ✓ Step one: The cheerleader holds the basic plank position for 10 seconds.
  - ✓ Step two: He rolls over to the side plank position on his right and holds for 10 seconds.
  - ✓ Step three: He returns back to the basic plank and holds again for 10.
  - ✓ Step four: He moves to the side plank position on his left and holds for 10.
  - ✓ The cheerleader repeats this set five times.

Coaching Points:
- The cheerleader should not arch his back or lift his hips too high causing the body to pike. The body needs to remain parallel to the floor. Body movement and shifting indicates the cheerleader has reached his limit in holding the plank.
- Check to make sure that the cheerleader breathes evenly through the drill and does not hold his breath.
- Plank exercises are isometric training, which involves contracting the muscles against a stationary resistance. They improve energy transmission between the upper body and lower body.
- Planking requires contraction though the abs, which is a needed skill applicable to tumbling, stunting, and jumping.
- These drills require focus in order to hold the proper form as long as possible. The focus helps to build concentration in your cheerleaders.
- Strengthening the entire body with one set of drills protects the cheerleader from injury.

Variations:

- In the basic plank position, the cheerleader slowly lifts one leg three to four inches off the floor and holds for five seconds then switches legs and repeats.
- Repeat the drill variation, but he lifts one arm straight out in front of him instead of the leg. The cheerleader continues the same pattern of holding for five seconds, and then he switches to the other arm.

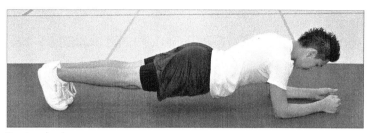

Basic plank

Side plank

Variation—leg lift

Variation—arm lift

#46: Pelvic Lift

Objective: To tone and strengthen the muscles in the lower back

Equipment Needed: Matted surface, box

Description:
- The cheerleader lies flat on her back with the feet supported on a step or small box about one foot off the ground.
- The cheerleader extends her arms straight overhead and beside her ears.
- Next, she tenses her glutes and pushes her heels into the box to lift her hips and back off the floor.
- The cheerleader pushes the back of her hands into the floor.
- The only point of contact with the floor will be her hands, arms, shoulders, and the back of the head.
- The cheerleader should feel tension in her gluts, lower back, and shoulders.
- Her body will be in an arched position.
- The cheerleader holds this position for 10 seconds.
- The cheerleader performs this drill 10 times.

Coaching Points:
- As the cheerleader gains strength, her shoulders will gradually begin to lift off the floor as well.
- Developing strength through the hips, back, legs, and abdominals helps to stabilize the body thus preventing injury.
- This drill is often prescribed to relieve lower back pain.

FLEXIBILITY DRILLS

Tumblers must be able to move their body parts through the broadest range of motion while maintaining stability in the joints. Stretching exercises for the shoulders, arms, back, and legs assist to increase range of motion and to help prevent muscle soreness. Working flexibility also aids cheerleaders' ability to perform gymnastic elements without causing injury due to tight muscles or improper balance of strength. Following are some drills specific for tumblers, but also check out flexibility drills in the both the stunting and jump chapters (Chapters 1 and 3) to improve elasticity through the muscles and joints.

#47: Wall Ball Roll

Objective: To increase range of motion in the wrists and develop fine motor skills

Equipment Needed: Wall, a tennis ball

Description:
- The cheerleader places the ball between the wall and her hand.
- With her palm open and fingers straight, the cheerleader rolls the ball in circles, using her hand and wrist, applying enough pressure so the ball does not fall.
- The cheerleader starts with small circles then increases the diameter of the circle; the bigger the circles, the harder it is to do.
- The cheerleader rolls the ball on the wall for 30 seconds. She reverses to the other hand and repeats.
- The cheerleader does three sets.

Coaching Point:
- Tightness through the wrists is one of the key problems in tumbling. This drill develops more flexibility and relieves tightness in the tendons around the wrist with less pressure on the joints because the cheerleader is not using both body weight and gravity as she does in tumbling.

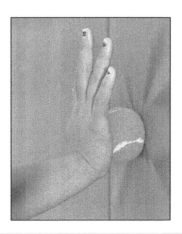

#48: Wrist/Forearm Stretch

Objective: To increase flexibility in the wrists and forearms

Equipment Needed: None

Description:
- The cheerleader starts in a kneeling position on the floor.
- The cheerleader clasps her hands together in front of the body and then opens them like a book.
- The cheerleader places her hands with the palms flat on the ground, her fingers facing toward her knees. She needs to keep them close to her knees.
- With her arms straight, the cheerleader leans backward, sitting into her legs, to stretch through the forearms and wrists.
- The cheerleader holds the position for 30 seconds.
- Next, the cheerleader rotates her fingers outward like a butterfly and gently rocks side to side for 30 seconds.
- Lastly, the cheerleader rotates her fingers to the front and leans forward, holding the stretch for 30 seconds.
- The cheerleader performs three sets.

Coaching Points:
- Stretching needs to be done slowly with no bouncing.
- As the cheerleader holds the stretch, the sensation of tightness should diminish. If not, tell the cheerleader to ease off slightly to a more comfortable stretch.
- If pain occurs, the cheerleader should stop the stretch immediately.
- The key to stretching for the cheerleader is to be relaxed while concentrating on the area being stretched.

#49: Wall Walks

Objective: To increase range of motion through the lower back

Equipment Needed: None

Description:
- The cheerleader starts with her back toward the wall, standing about two to three feet away.
- The cheerleader arches her back and reaches her hands to the wall behind her head.
- The cheerleader slowly, and in a controlled manner, walks her hands down the wall, bending through the back until she reaches the floor in a bridge position.
- In the bridge position, the cheerleader pushes her weight over her shoulders and hands.
- When the cheerleader reaches the floor or as low as she can go, she walks her hands back up the wall to the starting position.
- The cheerleader performs five sets.

Coaching Points:
- In the beginning, the cheerleader will need a spotter for safety and assistance until she can safety control her hands moving down the wall.
- This is a beginning drill that must be mastered by the cheerleader before she tries to do a back walkover.

#50: Wall Back Walkovers

Objective: To develop back flexibility and proper technique for a back walkover

Equipment Needed: Wall and padded mat

Description:
- The cheerleader faces the wall and sits on the floor with legs bent at the knees, and toes touching the base of the wall.
- The cheerleader lies back on the floor and places her hands palm down on the floor next to her head.
- The cheerleader pushes hips upward, forming a bridge.
- Her arms are straight.
- The cheerleader slowly steps her feet up the wall.
- At the top of the lift, her body will be diagonal to the wall, and the cheerleader kicks one leg over her body to the floor.
- Her other leg follows to the floor.
- The cheerleader finishes with a step out to a lunge.

Coaching Points:
- Have another cheerleader spotting this skill when a cheerleader is first working her way through it.
- It is crucial that the cheerleader has straight arms for both safety and clean technique.
- If the athlete cannot kick over, the cheerleader needs to start closer to the wall at the beginning of the drill.
- When the athlete becomes proficient at this drill, replace a panel mat for the wall and attempt the same drill.

3

Motion Drills

Strong, sharp motions are the trademark of cheerleading. Whether performing a chant, jumping to get the crowd motivated, dancing in a routine, or hitting a stunt, a perfectly formed motion elevates a teams' performance to the next level. Sharp, strong, and properly placed motions add uniformity and synchronicity to a cheer team. Motions come into play in all elements of cheer from sideline, to dances, stunting, and jumps. Using motion drills in everyday practices will develop strength in the arms and perfect proper technique. Not only is a cheer team with sharp motions and synchronized execution great to watch, but also a long-sought-after skill that all coaches would like their team to possess.

The cheerleaders need to learn the names for each move in order to understand and execute them properly. Types of arm motions include:

- High-V motion (Figure 3-1): Both arms are placed above the head in a V-position, slightly forward with elbows locked. The cheerleader must relax her shoulders and extend the arms through the wrists in a straight line. The hands are in a tight fist.

Figure 3-1. High-V motion

- Low-V motion (Figure 3-2): The arms extend down in front of body and slightly forward in an upside-down V-position with elbows locked. The hands are in a fist.

Figure 3-2. Low-V motion

- Touchdown or goalpost motion (Figure 3-3): The arms are extended straight above the head parallel to each other. The cheerleader squeezes her arms tight beside the head, and the hands are in a fist.

Figure 3-3. Touchdown or goalpost motion

- Low touchdown motion (Figure 3-4): This move is the same as a touchdown motion, except the arms are both extended down in front of the body.

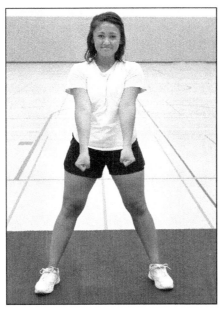

Figure 3-4. Low touchdown motion

- Clap motion (Figure 3-5): The cheerleader bends her arms and pulls her elbows together in front of her body. Her hands clap together with her fingers tight in what is called a blade position.

Figure 3-5. Clap motion

- Clasp motion (Figure 3-6): This motion is similar to the clap, except the fingers are cupped around each other.

Figure 3-6. Clasp motion

- Low clasp motion (Figure 3-7): Same motion as the clasp, except the arms are extended down in front of body.

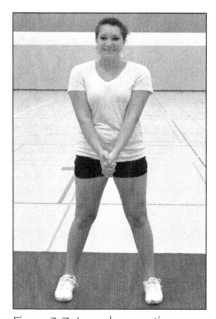

Figure 3-7. Low clasp motion

- Diagonal motion (Figure 3-8): One arm extends diagonally up, and the opposite arm extends diagonally down. The hands are in a fist. Arms are slightly forward and should form a direct diagonal line from wrist to wrist.

Figure 3-8. Diagonal motion

- Punch motion (Figure 3-9): One hand is placed on the hip in a fist and the opposite arm lifts directly overhead, close to the ear, with the elbow straight.

Figure 3-9. Punch motion

- K-motion (Figure 3-10): The cheerleader extends her left arm diagonally up and out as she places her right arm diagonally down and across her body.

Figure 3-10. K-motion

- L-motion (Figure 3-11): The cheerleader lifts her right arm straight up by the ear with the wrist facing in, and the left arm extends straight out to the left with the wrist facing down.

Figure 3-11. L-motion

- T-motion (Figure 3-12): The cheerleader places her arms straight out to her sides parallel to the floor. Her hands form a fist.

Figure 3-12. T-motion

- Broken-T or half-T motion (Figure 3-13): The cheerleader extends her arms out to the side and bends her elbows. Her fists come back to her shoulders.

Figure 3-13. Broken-T or half-T motion

- Bow-and-arrow motion (Figure 3-14): The cheerleader places one arm out to the side parallel to the floor, and the other arm bends at the elbow with her fist at her chest.

Figure 3-14. Bow-and-arrow motion

- Dagger motion (Figure 3-15): Cheerleader has her arms at her side close to her body. She bends her elbows, placing her fist at her shoulders.

Figure 3-15. Dagger motion

- Box motion/candlesticks (Figure 3-16): The cheerleader's arms are extended in front of her with her elbows bent, and hands are in a fist.

Figure 3-16. Box motion/candlesticks

- Overhead clasp motion (Figure 3-17): The cheerleader clasps her hands together and extends them directly over her head.

Figure 3-17. Overhead clasp motion

Teaching proper placement of each motion and vigilant repetition will develop these required skills. Cheerleaders need to understand placement, perfection, punch, pathway, and performance when learning the different motions. Everybody has the ability to punch a strong motion with proper training and perseverance. If a cheerleader practices these skills correctly, she will execute them correctly when performing.

TIMING AND TECHNIQUE DRILLS

Timing and technique are the essential keys to motion success. Using a variety of motion drills on a regular basis can add the stamina and knowledge needed to keep a cheerleader tight and focused.

Whenever beginning a motion drill, have cheerleaders stand with their feet shoulder-width apart, toes slightly turned out, and legs locked. Arms should be straight down by their side, chest up, shoulders back, and a tight core. Hands are in a tight fist, with the thumbs placed over the fingers.

#51: Wall Motion

Objective: To bring body awareness; to not swing or pull the arms behind the cheerleader's bodyline

Equipment Needed: Long, flat wall with no obstructions

Description:
- Position six to eight cheerleaders (depending on space availability) against a wall with heels approximately six inches away from wall.
- Select one cheerleader to stand in front of the line, facing the other cheerleaders. She is the line leader and calls the motion the cheerleaders will perform.
- The line leader calls the name of the motion, counts five, six, seven, eight, and then yells "hit."
- On the word "hit," the cheerleaders demonstrate the called motion in a well-placed manner, making sure their arms do not hit the wall at any time and are not positioned behind their bodies while holding the motion.
- The cheerleaders continue the sequence, covering all the cheerleading motions.

Coaching Points:
- Rotate the current line leader into the group of cheerleaders positioned against the wall and delegate another cheerleader to become the line leader. This gives each cheerleader an opportunity to lead the drill and also to visually see execution rights and wrongs.
- Line leaders gives the coach a chance to evaluate and correct the motions while the line leader calls the different motions.

#52: Hit It

Objective: To emphasis proper arm placement and angles; to synchronize the team

Equipment Needed: Large, spacious area with no obstructions

Description:
- Divide the cheerleaders into equal groups. Line them up in rows directly behind each other. Their legs are shoulder-width apart and hands clasped together in front of chest.
- Coach will call out a motion and then count one, two, three, and shout, "Hit it."
- All should sharply execute the called motion on the "hit it" command.
- Cheerleaders snap their arms to the correct position at the same time. The group should look like one unit, all moving at the same time and reaching the desired motion together.

Coaching Points:
- A coach should continually monitor the cheerleaders' proper stances and body alignments while conducting this drill, making sure their feet do not shift.
- Improper placement or poor timing is easier for a coach to spot when the team is in a row formation.
- This exercise develops strong motions and builds endurance and strength through repetition and concentration.
- View the drill from all angles to get a better perspective of entire team. This enables a coach to see the execution of the chosen motion and she can make the necessary changes.
- Check that the cheerleader's arms placements are slightly in front of the body.
- As the arms snap to position, they should not bobble or jiggle, but hit the exact location and freeze in that spot.

- When transitioning from one move to the next, the cheerleader should take the shortest distance with her arms to the next spot and wait until the last second to move quickly and precisely.
- The cheerleader should always be aware in what direction her fist is facing for each motion.
- For variety, this skill can also be done with the cheerleaders facing each other.

#53: Resistance

Objective: To aid the cheerleader's understanding of tight, strong arms when executing motions

Equipment Needed: Large, spacious area with no obstructions

Description:
- At random times, without any notice, the coach pushes on the cheerleader's arms during a motion practice to check to see if her arms are tight or limp. A cheerleader's arms should always be contracted.
- This drill reinforces to the cheerleader that her arms should be able to hold the motion with muscles engaged even when some resistance is applied from an outside force.

Coaching Points:
- Resistance checks are important because cheerleaders tend to relax their muscles while holding a position, making their form soft and angles off.
- When arms are not tight, timing and synchronization are off, making the team's moves look sloppy.

#54: Mirror Mirror

Objective: To have the cheerleader view and critic her own motions

Equipment Needed: Large mirror or reflective surface

Description:
- Cheerleaders divide up into pairs.
- One cheerleader calls a motion while the other cheerleader hits the position in front of the mirror.
- Together, they can evaluate and teach each other the proper form and alignment.

Coaching Points:
- A mirror is a valuable tool in understanding proper placement of arms for the cheerleaders.
- Often, cheerleaders think they are hitting the correct move based on the feel. By watching themselves in a mirror, they often can see that what they thought was correct placement was in reality incorrect.
- Often, cheerleaders do not realize that they are executing a motion incorrectly. Using this technique helps them better understand what they look like and how to correct their mistakes.

#55: Dumbbell Motions

Objective: To strengthen the upper body

Equipment Needed: Two-pound dumbbells, two weights per cheerleader

Description:
- Cheerleaders execute the following motions with a light weight in each hand: T-motion, high-V, low-V, touchdown, diagonal, punch, K-motion, right L-motion, left L-motion, broken-T, and daggers.
- Cheerleaders perform three reps per motion.

Coaching Points:
- The cheerleader must tighten her core in order to isolate the muscles used to perform correct motions.
- Check for proper body alignment while lifting weights. Cheerleaders should not lift their shoulders or round their backs while lifting the weights.
- Do not let the cheerleader swing the weight, but rather place it in the proper position.

#56: Broomstick

Objective: To give a reference location for high-Vs and low-Vs

Equipment Needed: Broomstick/dowel rod cut to a length that is equal to the distance between hands in a high/low-V

Description:
- The cheerleader hits a high-V.
- Place the dowel between her hands.
- With her hands in a fist, the cheerleader presses inward on the dowel from both ends so that it is held in place. She cannot grip the dowel with her hands.
- The cheerleader practices going from high-V to low-V positions without dropping the stick.
- One movement from high-V to low-V is one set.
- Each cheerleader performs 10 sets.

Coaching Points:
- The muscle contraction adds tension to the arms and increases the cheerleader's shoulder and arm strength.
- This drill teaches the cheerleader that tension is needed in the arms when executing these moves. It will eliminate loose, sloppy motions in cheers and dance moves.
- This exercise targets the muscles used during these motions. Through repetition, muscle memory develops.

Variation:
- Place a rope between the cheerleader's arms that are in a high-V position.
- The cheerleader wraps the ends of the rope around her fists.
- While gripping the rope, she pulls it so that there is no slack in the middle.
- The cheerleader repeats the same movements as listed above with the piece of rope extended between her arms that are in a high-V.
- The cheerleader performs 10 sets.

#57: M-O-T-I-O-N

Objective: To develop muscle memory and proper arm placement in a friendly competitive environment

Equipment Needed: Spacious room/gym

Description:
- Cheerleaders stand in a line where they can easily see the person in front of them. This drill is a "follow the leader" type exercise.
- The first cheerleader performs a two eight-count motion sequence.
- The second cheerleader replicates the exact sequence of the first cheerleader.
- If the second cheerleader succeeds, the third cheerleader repeats the same sequence and the challenge continues down the row.
- If the second cheerleader does not repeat the sequence correctly, then she will receive the letter "M." The third cheerleader would then create a completely new sequence.
- Proceed through all of the cheerleaders.
- For every sequence that cannot be repeated, a letter from the word M-O-T-I-O-N is added to the individual cheerleader who fails to properly duplicate the sequence demonstrated before her.
- The object of the game is to not get a letter from the word M-O-T-I-O-N. If a cheerleader collects all the letters, then she is out of the game. The winner is the last cheerleader left.

Coaching Points:
- The coach should oversee that each cheerleader performs the sequence correctly.
- Confirm that they are using a wide variety of motions during the sequences in order to strengthen all parts of the arm and shoulders.

- Moves need to be performed accurately with sharp, crisp arm placements. Often, cheerleaders tend to rush through the pattern causing them to execute sloppy motions.
- Remind cheerleaders that this is a friendly game to strengthen their motions and memory. Some athletes get caught up in the competitive nature of the exercise and lose the sense of fun.
- If working on a time constraint, substitute a shorter word to shorten the game.

#58: Jumping Jills

Objective: To warm up the muscles, develop proper motion technique, and develop cardiovascular fitness

Equipment Needed: Large space

Description:
- This drill is very similar to a jumping jack except cheerleading motions are done when the feet are apart.
- Cheerleaders starts with feet together and arms at their sides.
- All moves are done to counts of eight.
- The coach starts the sequence by yelling, "Five, six, seven, eight."
- On count one, the cheerleader dips slightly through her knees and jumps her feet apart to a wide stance, hitting a high-V with her arms on count two.
- On count three, the cheerleader returns her feet together and arms to her side.
- On count four, the cheerleader hops her feet apart and her arms hit a low-V position.
- On count five, the cheerleader brings her feet and arms back together.
- On count six, the cheerleader hits a diagonal position as her feet jump apart again.
- On count seven, the cheerleader hops her feet together as in count one.
- On count eight, the cheerleader jumps her feet apart, and she hits a right arm punch and her left hand is on her hip.
- The cheerleader will repeat the pattern executing all the different cheerleading arm position listed when her feet are in a wide stance.
    - ✓ High/low-Vs
    - ✓ Ts/broken-Ts
    - ✓ Punches
    - ✓ Daggers
    - ✓ Touchdown
    - ✓ Fist, blades

Coaching Points:
- Cheerleaders must use sharp, accurate motion placement during this exercise. Usually, jumping jacks are very fluid and casual. Cheerleaders need to hit the motion with precision and proper technique at the top of the jumping jill.
- When the legs are apart, the feet need to be slightly turned out with the knees bending directly over the toes when executing the hopping in and out.

- This exercise not only builds aerobic fitness, but also muscular response for speed of movement. When the feet hit the floor during the jumping process, the quadriceps muscle shortens, and then a rapid stretch follows when the next jump is performed, causing a stretch-shorten cycle. This process increases power production, strengthen bones, and increases movement speed.

4

Stunt Drills

Stunting is the lifting or throwing of a cheerleader into the air by one or more people with their feet in contact with the performance surface. Stunting defies gravity. Stunts range from thigh stands to fully extended heel stretches to mile-high basket tosses. Most cheerleaders will tell you stunting is the best part of cheerleading. Stunting is by far the part that cheerleaders want to focus on the most. They enjoy the challenge, teamwork, and accomplishments achieved when stunting. It takes team effort to perfect the desired skills. Cheerleaders have to develop a working relationship that stresses strength, knowledge, safety, and ability.

A qualified coach must be trained and certified in stunting for the protection and safety of their cheerleaders. A good instructional course should include both book and hands-on training in order for the coach to learn the proper procedures and technique for building stunts and pyramids. Check with your local organization or state to find a good place to become stunt-certified.

All stunts must be taught in progression, working step by step from the basics to the more advanced levels. To do this, a coach should make a list of the stunt goals that the team wants to achieve, and then break them down into stunt progressions. A common phrase heard in cheerleading is: "Perfection before progression." Every person should understand and master the proper procedures for building thigh stands and prep/elevators before advancing onto extended advanced stunts. The best way to achieve and verify these skills is through documentation with a stunt progression chart. Stunting is a high-risk activity. Each element must be practiced and perfected at the lowest level before moving onto shoulder and overhead levels. Proper technique has to be developed for both the bases and top person/flyer.

A stunt group has four positions:

- *Base:* The person in the stunt who remains in contact with the floor, and lifts a top person/flyer into a stunt/mount. She is the foundation of the stunt. Stunts can be executed with one base under the top person/flyer, but most often group stunting has two bases. Bases are defined as a main base or secondary base.
- *Back spotter:* The person who has direct contact with the performing surface and whose primary responsibility is the safety of the top person/flyer by protecting her head, neck, and shoulder area. The back spotter often assists with building the stunt.
- *Top person/flyer:* The person who is elevated into the air by the base(s). She must control her body, keeping it straight, tight, and aligned with the bases. Her eyes are looking forward and head is in a neutral position, looking forward.
- *Front spotter/front base:* The person placed in the front to help build a stunt. Most often, she provides support around the wrists of the bases as they lift the top person/flyer. This is an extra person and is not required to build a stunt.

The coach determines what position each athlete performs in order to meet the needs of the team. Often, athletes want to be a top person/flyer or front spotter. They also want to choose their own stunt group, picking their friends or the best top person/flyer on the team to be in their group but it is imperative that the coach makes the final decisions on positions. As the coach, you need to know what skills are needed in order to properly perform certain physical skills. Evaluate each athlete individually to match their strength and skills to the position that fits their abilities. Each cheerleader must develop the understanding and capability to adequately perform the skills.

Stunts range from two-legged to one-legged skills performed by a person that is supported in the air by one to four people.

Basic stunts are as follows:
- Prep/elevator (Figure 4-1): Typically performed with four athletes: right/main base, left/secondary base, top person/flyer, and back spotter. Both bases stand facing each other with legs apart in an A-frame structure. They support the top person/flyer in their hands with wrist together at chest level. The top person/flyer stands tall with feet approximately shoulder-width apart, shifting her weight evenly between the bases. The back spotter's primary job is to protect the head, neck, and shoulders of the top person/flyer. Her eyes must never leave the top person/flyer. She may choose to maintain contact with the top person/flyer at several locations: ankles, calves, or thighs.

Figure 4-1. Prep/elevator

- Full extension (Figure 4-2): Similar to the prep/elevator, except the bases hold the top person/flyer completely extended above their heads with straight arms. The job for the top person/flyer is exactly the same as in the prep/elevator. The back spotter must be aggressive in maintaining safety since this skill is at a higher risk level due to its increased height. It is highly recommend having a back spotter that is taller than both bases to allow her to reach the top person/flyer's ankles when building the stunt and sustaining safety.

Figure 4-2. Full extension

- Liberty (Figure 4-3): Typically performed with four athletes. This extended stunt requires the primary and secondary bases to lift the top person/flyer into the air by holding under one of her feet with a liberty grip. The top person/flyer stands tall on one foot. The other foot is lifted up and set directly by the straight leg's knee. The back spotter's primary job is safety. She grips tightly around the top person/flyer's support ankle with both hands. In the event the top person/flyer falls, the back spotter helps to catch the top person/flyer with emphasis on protecting the top person/flyer's neck, head, and shoulders.

Figure 4-3. Liberty

- Coed stunt (Figure 4-4): This skill has one base, top person/flyer and a back spotter for safety. The base holds the top person/flyer at her waist while she grasps around his wrist. The top person/flyer is tossed into the air by the base, and he catches her at the top. She can be in a chair, shoulder-level hands, or fully extended one- or two-legged position.

Figure 4-4. Coed stunt

- Basket toss/straight ride (Figure 4-5): This skill is usually done with five athletes: right base, left base, top person/flyer, front base/spotter, and back spotter. The two bases interweave their hands forming a basket toss grip. The basket grip provides the platform for the top person/flyer to place her feet. The top person/flyer loads her feet into the bases' hands. The bases together with the help of the back spotter and front spotter toss the top person/flyer into the air.

Figure 4-5. Basket toss/straight ride

Stunt positions and grips go hand in hand. In order to build the stunts, bases need to know the proper hand position or grip. The primary grips are as follows:

- Standard prep/elevator grip (Figure-4-6): Each base forms a platform with their hands for the top person/flyer to put her feet. The top person/flyer places her right foot into the primary base's hand. She loads into the primary base's hand, and then puts her left foot into the secondary base's hand. The back spotter has several choices for grip placement. The most common position is at each ankle.

Figure 4-6. Standard prep/elevator grip

- Standard extension grip (Figure 4-7): Bases' hands form a platform under the shoe of the top person/flyer with the fingers gripping the heel and toe of the shoe. The top person/flyer's feet are held fully extended with both bases' arm straight over their heads. The back spotter grips the top person/flyer's ankles.

Figure 4-7. Standard extension grip

- Standard liberty grip (Figure 4-8): The grips are described as if the top person/flyer is doing a right-leg liberty. The primary base's hands form a platform under the top person/flyer's right shoe with her wrists far enough apart for the secondary base to place her right hand under middle of the top person/flyer's shoe. The secondary base's left hand is placed in one of several locations (but not limited to): gripping the main base's right wrist, gripping the top of the top person/flyer's foot, or placing her hand over the primary base's hands. The back spotter grasps around the top person/flyer's ankle.

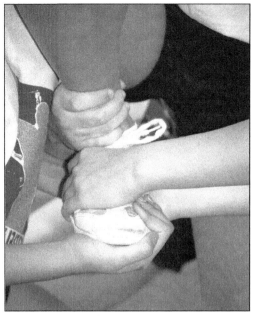

Figure 4-8. Standard liberty grip

- Basket grip (Figure 4-9): With their right hand, both bases will grasp their own left wrist. At the same time, with their left hand, both bases grasp the other's right wrist. The front spotter and back spotter place their hands directly under the bases' interweaved basket grip.

In order to build stunts, cheerleaders must be trained in the following areas:
- Trust
- Strength
- Technique and timing
- Flexibility

Figure 4-9. Basket grip

TRUST DRILLS

As a team, every member must trust, understand, and commit to one another. Each stunt is usually composed of four members. They have to rely on each other and work together as one unit in order to build safe, properly executed stunts. It is like a mini-team within a larger team. Team-building activities, bonding games, and basic-level stunting drills with emphasis on stunt progression create confidence and trust for both your top person/flyer and the bases.

#59: Trust Falls

Objective: To develop trust and proper technique between the top person/flyer and the base group

Equipment Needed: One sturdy box or bench

Description:
- A stunt group consisting of two bases, a top person/flyer, and a back spotter is used in this drill.
- Step 1
  - ✓ The top person/flyer stands in front of the bases and back spotter. She faces away from them with her arms at her side and her feet together.
  - ✓ The bases extend their arms toward the top person/flyer and on a designated count; she falls back into their arms.
  - ✓ The bases catch her and then place her back to the starting position.
  - ✓ They perform this set three times, and then move on to Step 2.
- Step 2
  - ✓ The stunt group performs the same drill, but this time the top person/flyer stands on a box with her arms crossed at her chest.
  - ✓ The top person/flyer falls back into the arms of the bases and back spotter.
  - ✓ The bases absorb the downward momentum of the catch with their legs.
  - ✓ The back spotter catches under the armpits of the top person/flyer.
  - ✓ The team implements this drill five times, and then moves on to Step 3.
- Step 3
  - ✓ The top person/flyer is on the box with her arms in a T-motion. Her feet are together, and her body is tight.
  - ✓ The top person/flyer dips through her legs and jumps back into the bases' arms.
  - ✓ As she lands in their arms, the top person/flyer catches the bases' shoulders with her hands.
  - ✓ The back spotter scoops under the top person/flyer's arms during the catch.

Coaching Points:
- The top person/flyer must not look behind her before she executes this drill. She understands to trust that the group will be there to catch her when she is cradled, tossed, or falls.
- The top person/flyer keeps her body tight with her legs and feet together. As she lands in the bases' arms, she must remain tight. It is far easier for the bases to catch a falling top person/flyer when she stays tight like a board versus loose like a rubber band or wet noodle. Also, staying tight prevents the bases and back spotter from getting hit by flying arms and legs.
- Once the team understands the concept of trust, they will only need to do Step 3 to reinforce correct cradling technique for the top person/flyer and bases.

#60: Bear Hug

Objective: To develop trust for the top person/flyer that the bases will catch her; to teach the bases proper catching techniques

Equipment Needed: One sturdy box or bench

Description:
- The top person/flyer stands on a bench or bottom row of a bleacher with her hands clasped together and her arms extended diagonally in front of her body.
- Two bases stand on either side of top person/flyer and reach up and catch her in a tight hug position, pulling the top person/flyer close to their bodies and lifting her upward during the catch called resisting.
- The bases catch the top person/flyer in midair so the top person/flyer's feet do not land on the floor.
- The top person/flyer keeps her body tight and arms clasped.

Coaching Points:
- Humans have a natural survival instinct and will often try to cover their face or body when something or someone is coming toward them. This drill reinforces a "catch reaction" for the bases rather then a "run reaction."
- The bases need to stay close to the top person/flyer and be ready to catch her. Their arms need to be tight and contracted before she lands in their arms. If the arms are relaxed or too low, the top person/flyer could be caught too near the ground, causing possible injury.

#61: The Caterpillar

Objective: To aid the top person/flyer's understanding of maintaining a strong, tight body position while stunting; to add an element of fun to practice

Equipment Needed: None

Description:
- Seven or more cheerleaders lie on their backs on the floor, side by side, and alternating their head and feet.
- Their heads are aligned, their arms are extended toward the ceiling, and their knees are bent to keep them stable.
- A separate cheerleader lies down onto the hands of the cheerleaders on the floor.
- The cheerleaders on the floor pass her down the row of hands to the opposite end.

Coaching Points:
- The more cheerleaders lying on the floor, the more fun it is.
- For safety, assign a spotter to follow the cheerleader on the side as she is being passed down the row.
- Playing team-bonding games like this one serves double duty. It is a great way for the team to have fun and to learn to trust each other.
- Explain to the team how the cheerleader can safely and easily be moved down the row of hands because she maintained a tight body position. Relate this same principle to a top person/flyer, explaining it is the same as when she is being lifted into the air in a stunt.
- This is a low-risk game that the cheerleaders can easily equate to stunting.

STRENGTHENING DRILLS

Studies have shown that adding resistance to a workout greatly enhances muscular strength and muscle balance. Building strength in the legs, back, arms, and shoulders can be developed with resistance bands, medicine ball, free weights, and lifting each other. Using a variety of equipment prevents boredom in the cheerleader's workout. Having a well-planned strengthening program not only increases strength, but also develops explosive power, endurance, and muscle tone that will enable the cheerleaders to build elite-level stunts and pyramids.

If your school has a trainer on staff, ask him to organize a strength workout that the cheerleaders can do to augment their training regiment.

Resistance Band Drills

Rubberized resistance bands are also called tension bands, therapy bands, and exercise bands. They can be purchased in rolls and cut to the desired length. Eight-foot band length is best for the exercises described in this book. They also come in different resistance from light to heavy. Having a variety of resistance can enhance the effectiveness of the drills. Often, these stretchy bands are used for physical therapy. For strengthening the muscle groups, use a lighter resistance band in the beginning with more reps and then have the cheerleaders work toward the heavier resistance ones and use fewer reps.

#62: Seated Row

Objective: To strengthen the upper back and shoulders in order to lift another person into the air safely during the stunting process

Equipment Needed: Resistance bands

Description:
- The cheerleader begins sitting on the floor with her legs and arms extended straight in front of her. She wraps the ends of the band around her hands and loops the center of the band around the balls of the feet.
- The cheerleader pulls her arms back toward her torso with her palms facing down, opening out the elbows on count one.
- On count two, the cheerleader extends her arms straightforward.
- On count three, the cheerleader pulls back her elbows, but this time, they are pointing down to the floor and tight to her side, the hands are at the waist with palms facing up.
- The arms extend forward again on counts four.
- On count five, six, seven, eight, keeping her elbows tight to her side, she curls her arms up and down twice (biceps curls).
- The cheerleader performs eight sets.

Coaching Points:
- For more stability, the cheerleader can slightly bend her knees, in order to maintain a tight core and straight back.
- Have the cheerleader walk through the sequence without the bands to get an understanding of proper placement of the arms and hands.
- The cheerleader should squeeze her shoulder blades together when pulling back on the bands.
- The eight-count sequence needs to be done slowly and controlled for maximum benefit. She should control the band rather than allowing the band to control her.
- The cheerleader should avoid hyperextending or overflexing the joints when using the bands.
- Have the cheerleader breathe evenly while doing the moves. Often, cheerleaders hold their breathe during the exertion.

#63: Arabesque Biceps Curls

Objective: To strengthen shoulders and arms; to increase balance for the top person/flyer

Equipment Needed: Resistance bands

Description:
- The top person/flyer wraps the ends of the band around her hands.
- The top person/flyer places one foot in front of the body and steps onto the middle of the band.
- The elbows of the top person/flyer are bent at her side with her fists by her shoulders in a dagger motion.
- The top person/flyer leans forward placing all her weight on the front leg and lifts the back leg straight behind her, hitting an arabesque position.
- Holding that position with her body and legs, the top person/flyer does bicep curls with her arms. The goal is to balance on one leg in an arabesque position as she executes the curls.
- The top person/flyer performs five bicep curls for one set.
- The top person/flyer does five sets.

Coaching Points:
- The cheerleader needs to keep her hips and shoulders squared to the floor and her core contracted.
- Hitting the arabesque position first is key to performing this drill.
- If the cheerleader is having a hard time with balance, try the drill without the bands. Once this step is perfected, then add the band section back to the drill.
- Encourage the cheerleader to not wobble as she curls her arms. Perfecting this skill on the floor develops muscle memory for the cheerleader so she can execute proper form of an arabesque while extended in a stunt with a variety of arm motions.

#64: Reverse Torso Curls

Objective: To strengthen the core and lower back

Equipment Needed: Resistance bands

Description:
- The cheerleader sits on the floor with legs extended in front of her and the band wrapped around the feet.
- Gripping the ends of the bands with her hands, the cheerleader slowly lowers her body backward to the floor while contracting her core muscles.
- About halfway down, the cheerleader holds the position for 10 to 30 seconds. Her ultimate goal is to do this skill for one minute.
- The cheerleader performs five repetitions for one set.
- The cheerleader does five sets.

Coaching Points:
- Core strength is needed for bases not only to safely build elite-level stunts, but to develop a strong mid-section that will prevent injury to the back.
- For a top person/flyer, a strong core gives her the ability to hold a straight-body position in the air as well as develop good balance.

#65: Triceps Pull

Objective: To lengthen and strengthen the triceps

Equipment Needed: Resistance bands

Description:
- The cheerleader places the band behind her back.
- The cheerleader holds on to the top of the band with her right arm by her ear and her left hand by the lower left side of her back and grabs the bottom of the band.
- Stabilizing with her left hand, the cheerleader slowly extends the band with her right arm upward as high as possible on the diagonal to a count of one through four.
- The cheerleader then returns her right arm back down to the starting position on counts five through eight.
- The cheerleader performs five repetitions with her right arm.
- The cheerleader switches so her left arm is positioned at the top of her left shoulder and her right hand at her right lower back.
- The cheerleader does five repetitions with her left arm.
- The cheerleader does three sets.

Coaching Points:
- The cheerleader should not bend her wrists when pulling on the band. It causes too much stress on the ligaments.
- To protect the back, the cheerleader must tighten her core and straighten her back. Check that she does not bend at the waist while extending the arm.
- The triceps do most of the pushing movements in the arms and, therefore, must be strengthen in order to push a person upward while stunting.

#66: Biceps Curls

Objective: To strengthen the biceps and balance the muscle groups in the arms for the bases

Equipment Needed: Resistance bands

Description:
- The cheerleader places the band on the floor and steps with her feet together in the middle of the band.
- The cheerleader wraps the ends of the band around the palms of the hand.
- With her elbows tucked into her side and wrists straight, the cheerleader curls her hands, palms up, slowly toward her chest.
- The cheerleader slowly returns her hands back to her side.
- The cheerleader performs 10 reps for each set.
- The cheerleader does three sets.

Coaching Points:
- In the beginning, the cheerleader needs to start with the lightest resistance band in order to maintain proper body technique. Using too strong of a band can force the athlete to bend her lower back in order to lift the bands to the chest.
- Often, the cheerleader will not be able to pull the band completely up to her chest. Stress that is okay, so she will work progressively to that goal.
- To do a proper biceps curl, the cheerleader should have no motion through her shoulders or back, only in her arms.
- The cheerleader does not bend her wrists during the curls.
- Biceps curls can also be done with a pair of free weights instead of the resistance band.

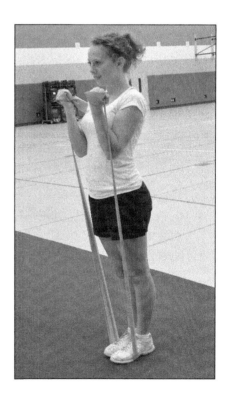

#67: Base Building

Objective: To strengthen the arms and legs; to simulate the proper movement and feel of building a prep or elevator stunt

Equipment Needed: Resistance bands

Description:
- The cheerleader places the band flat on the floor.
- The cheerleader steps on the band with her feet shoulder-width apart.
- The cheerleader grabs the band with a secure grip by wrapping the ends around her palms.
- The cheerleader places her arms in a load-in position with elbows tucked tight to the body and hands at belly button level. Her knees are bent.
- The cheerleader fully extends her arms over her head, keeping her arms by her ears, as she straightens her legs.
- The cheerleader carefully returns her arms back the starting position.
- This drill is done to two eight-counts, simulating a load-in to a fully extended stunt.
- On count one, two, the cheerleader dips by bending her knees. On three, four, she extends her arms overhead, on count five, six, her arms hit the top, and on count seven, eight, she holds her arms in the fully extended position.
- For the second eight-count, the cheerleader dips through her legs on count one, two, keeping her arms extended in the air. On count three, four, she straightens her legs and shrugs her shoulders. On count five, six, she lowers her arms back to the belly button position; holding it there for count seven, eight.
- The cheerleader performs eight sets.

Coaching Points:
- Monitor the cheerleader for correct posture and leg position. Her back should be straight and her shoulders engaged.
- Have the cheerleader walk through the steps without the bands to assure proper understanding and technique.
- In the beginning, start with the lightest resistance band in order to not strain the muscles and joints.

121

#68: Lean Shoulder Shrug Squat

Objective: To strengthen and tone the shoulders, core, and legs

Equipment Needed: Resistance bands

Description:
- The band is laying flat on the floor.
- The cheerleader steps on the middle of the band with her feet shoulder-width apart as she bends down and grabs the ends.
- The cheerleader slowly stands up keeping her abdominals tucked in.
- On count one, two, with her hands at her side and tension in the bands, she slowly leans to her right side.
- On count three, four, she returns back to the original standing position, centering her body over her legs.
- On count five, six, seven, eight, she shrugs her shoulders up to the ears and back down twice.
- On the second count of one through eight, she squats down and up four times.
- The cheerleader repeats the entire two eight-count sequence but this time, she leans to her left side.
- The cheerleader does eight sets.

Coaching Points:
- Knees remain soft (slightly bent) when leaning to the side and performing the shoulder shrugs in order to not hyperextend the knee joint.
- The exercise is simple but an excellent way to develop proper body alignment while strengthening many parts of the body from head to toe.

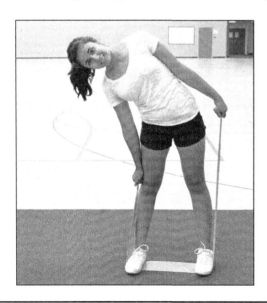

Dumbbell Drills

Doing drills with dumbbells increases the range of motion in the muscles and balances the muscle groups in the body. Dumbbells provide the ability for the cheerleader to perform dynamic, power-based movements. Following is a set of drills that a cheerleader can do to help them perform stunts better and safer. In addition, the drills on the following list can also be done with dumbbells:

- #11: Split Squats
- #18: Hop Across the Floor
- #38: Wall Sit
- #40: Serratus Punch
- #51: Wall Motions
- #66: Bicep Curls
- #67: Base Building
- #76: Step Lock
- #77: Standing Balance Board

#69: Chest Flies

Objective: To strengthen the pectoral muscles

Equipment Needed: Pair of dumbbells, matted surface

Description:
- With a dumbbell in each hand, the cheerleader lies on her back of the floor, her knees bent and arms extended out to her side.
- The cheerleader slowly lifts the weights up and together over her chest, palms facing toward each other, and keeping her arms straight.
- Ten reps equal one set.
- The cheerleader performs five sets.

Coaching Points:
- The cheerleader's back remains stationary and tight to the floor throughout the drill.
- Moving the weights slowly helps build muscles and give the body an improved workout because it forces the muscles to stabilize and support the weight in every phrase of the movement for a longer period of time.
- The wrists stay in alignment with the arms to prevent strain on the ligaments and possible injury.
- This exercise works both pushing and pulling, which is part of the stunting process.

#70: Arm Circles

Objective: To strengthen the shoulders and trapezoids

Equipment Needed: Pair of dumbbells

Description:
- With a dumbbell in each hand, the cheerleader stands with feet comfortably apart, and arms extended out to her side, parallel to the floor.
- The cheerleader slowly makes 12-inch circles forward with her arms, 10 times.
- The cheerleader circles backward with her arms, 10 times.
- Ten reps in each direction equals one set.
- The cheerleader performs three sets.

Coaching Points:
- The cheerleader performs the movements without weights to assure proper body alignment. Once mastered, she can add light weights to her arms.
- The cheerleader's back is straight with the abdominals and lower back muscles engaged.
- The wrists stay in alignment with the arms to prevent strain on the ligaments and possible injury.

Variation:
- Have the cheerleader turn her hands in different directions to work different muscles in the arm. For example, if she turns her thumbs to point up, she works the front portion of her shoulder muscles.

Medicine Ball Drills

The following drills use a medicine ball and sport-specific movements. These balls are a great way to exercise the entire body. Medicine ball training is suitable for all fitness levels. They improve range of motion, coordination, flexibility, joint integrity, explosive power, and strength. They focus on speed contraction of the muscles, and because they are relatively light, they allow the athlete to execute the drill explosively. It is best to have several sizes and weights in order to maximize the benefits of these drills. The cheerleader should begin with a lighter weight ball when first learning an exercise and only progress to a heavier ball as the drill is mastered.

#71: Ball Toss

Objective: To develop explosive power in the legs and arms as well as perfecting proper technique for cheerleaders who base stunts

Equipment Needed: Medicine ball

Description:
- A cheerleader starts with the medicine ball cupped in her hands at her shoulders and pulls her elbows tight to her side. Her feet are shoulder-width apart.
- On a designated count, the cheerleader bends her knees to a 90-degree angle and propels the ball directly over her head and into the air as she straightens her legs and arms.
- The cheerleader catches the ball and immediately bends her knees and arms, absorbing the downward momentum.
- The cheerleader does 10 repetitions.

Coaching Points:
- This drill mirrors the sport-specific techniques used in basic stunting. Practicing with a medicine ball gives the base the feel of propelling a cheerleader in the air. The cheerleader learns the need to use both her arms and legs when lifting or throwing a cheerleader overhead.

- The cheerleader throws by following through and fully extending the arms at the top.
- The cheerleader must always keep her eyes on the ball. Same idea is applied to stunting: a base must always keep her eyes on her top person/flyer.
- When the ball is free from the cheerleader's hands, she must still keep her arms and shoulders contracted.
- The cheerleader keeps the arms extended until the ball makes contact again with the hands and, then returns to the start position, absorbing the ball's downward momentum in her legs.

#72: Partner Ball Toss

Objective: To develop explosive power in the arms and shoulders for bases

Equipment Needed: Medicine ball

Description:
- Two cheerleaders stand about eight feet apart, facing each other.
- Holding the ball at shoulder level, one cheerleader dips through her legs and throws the ball up and toward her partner.
- With her arms extended, the second cheerleader catches the ball, bends her arms and her knees, absorbing the downward momentum through her legs.
- The second cheerleader immediately explodes from the legs and arms and throws the ball up and back to her partner.
- Throwing from one partner and back is a set.
- The group performs 10 sets.

Coaching Points:
- This drill not only simulates proper lifting and throwing technique used in stunting, but also stresses the importance of timing between two people. Cheerleaders learn that timing is as important as strength when stunting.
- Tossing a ball back and forth improves hand-eye coordination.
- When tossing, have the partner vary the tempo of the toss, which in turn teaches quick reflexes.
- The size of medicine ball can be tailored to the cheerleader's strength. Start with a lighter weight ball, and then add speed to the drill. Once mastered by the cheerleader, then she can perform drill with a heavier medicine ball.
- Another way to change up the drill is increase the distance between the cheerleaders. More power in the toss is needed in order to get the ball to the partner, thus increasing quickness and speed.

Variation—Push-Up Ball Toss:
- Start with two cheerleaders facing each other about eight feet apart.
- They sit on their knees with their torsos in an upright position.
- One cheerleader starts by holding the medicine ball at chest level.
- This cheerleader chest presses the medicine ball up and over to her partner.
- As she releases the ball, the first cheerleader falls forward onto her hands to the floor and immediately performs a push-up.
- The second cheerleader catches the ball and waits for the first cheerleader to complete the push-up before tossing the ball back.
- They repeat this process back and forth to each other for 20 repetitions.

- Make this drill more challenging by quickening the tempo of the back-and-forth toss. Have the cheerleader throw the ball immediately back to her partner. The partner will need to explode up from the push-up position so that she is back in the seated upright pose on her knees in time to catch the ball.

Variation—Push-Up Ball Toss

#73: Medicine Ball Circle

Objective: To strengthen the abdominals, lower back, and sides

Equipment Needed: Medicine ball

Description:
- Several cheerleaders form a circle, facing inward. They stand with their feet shoulder-width apart.
- Holding the ball with both hands, the cheerleaders pass the ball from one cheerleader to another around the circle, only twisting from the waist.
- They must keep their feet firmly planted on the floor.
- They need to also tighten their core muscles in order to maximize proper usage of the muscles.
- They pass the ball around the circle 10 times.
- Reverse the direction of the ball circle, and have the cheerleading group complete 10 circles in the new direction.

Coaching Points:
- Have the cheerleaders be mindful of their posture: shoulders down, pelvis tucked in, and feet firmly on the floor.
- This fun exercise simulates the twisting movements done in advanced stunting transitions.
- Strong backs and core muscles are essential while stunting. This drill increases the muscular strength without putting excess strain on the back.
- Often, cheerleaders want to speed up this drill, but it should be done at a moderate speed in order to produce maximum benefits.

#74: Medicine Ball Oblique Twist

Objective: To strengthen the abdominals, lower back and sides

Equipment Needed: Medicine ball, a mat

Description:
- A cheerleader lies on her back on the mat with her knees bent. She squeezes the ball between her knees. Her arms are extended out to the side and flat on the floor.
- Keeping her back on the floor, the cheerleader slowly lowers her knees to her right side, keeping the ball tight between her knees.
- The cheerleader slowly returns to the starting position with her knees up.
- Next, the cheerleader rotates her knees to her left side, squeezing the ball as his lowers her legs.
- The cheerleader executes two sets of 10 reps.

Coaching Points:
- The cheerleader must keep her shoulders, arms, hands, and upper back tight to the floor throughout the exercise.
- The cheerleader must resist gravity when her legs are moving toward the floor.
- On the returning of the knees to the upright position, the cheerleader cannot use momentum.
- Oblique training serves as a core stabilizer, which is paramount in good stunt technique.
- The oblique muscles are vital in supporting the torso and back, permitting rotation and flexibility.
- The cheerleader only needs to use lighter weight to train the obliques. This muscle group is being used all the time to stabilize the frame so once a week with lightweights is the best training for strength and stability.

TECHNIQUE AND TIMING DRILLS

In order for a group of cheerleaders to build a good and safe stunt, each person has to learn the proper technique and timing for her individual position. Each position requires not only strength, but also body awareness, balance, teamwork, synchronization, and strength. This section is broken into drills for the top person/flyer, bases, and spotters, and the stunt group working as one unit.

Top Person/Flyer Technique Drills

Body awareness is key to being a good top person/flyer. The following drills teach her to manipulate her body into the correct position to maintain proper balance and alignment through low-risk exercises. Using these drills will give her confidence and knowledge to fly in fully extended stunts safely.

#75: Cradle Hold

Objective: To teach body awareness for the top person/flyer when cradling

Equipment Needed: Large matted surface

Description:
- Four people are needed for this drill: two bases, a top person/flyer, a back spotter.
- The bases hold the top person/flyer in a cradle position.
- As the back spotter maintains contact with the top person/flyer by holding under her armpits, the side bases release the top person/flyer's legs with their front arms.
- The top person/flyer holds a pike body pose with her legs together and her toes pointed with no support from the bases.
- The top person/flyer sustains this position for five seconds working her way to 30 seconds.

Coaching Points:

- This drill stresses the importance to the top person/flyer that she must maintain a tight, controlled body while landing in a cradle. Many times, when a top person/flyer lands in the arms of the bases, she relaxes her body. A loose body is hard to catch and control. This drill reinforces the idea that a top person/flyer is an important part of the catching process and must do her part for both safety and proper technique.
- This drill also teaches the top person/flyer to use her abdominals to maintain the V-position or pike when cradling instead of depending on the bases to hold her in that position.

#76: Step Lock

Objective: To teach top person/flyer to have a tight, squared, controlled, aligned body

Equipment Needed: Stunt pedestal

- The pedestal is built with a wooden 2' x 2' x 2" thick base (approx), 1' x 0.75" pipe nipple, 2.75" pipe flanges, a 2" x 4" x 6" wooden step, four 2" x 0.25" bolts/nuts, four 1" lag bolts, and eight 1" flathead wood screws.
- The base is built of two pieces of 2x10 cut 18.5" and held together by mounting on a 3/8" piece of plywood using the flat head wood screws. The result is an 18.25" square, 2" high.
- The flange is centered in the base and held by four 0.25" bolts with washers and nuts countersunk into the plywood to make a smooth bottom surface so as not to tear a mat or scar a wood floor.
- Edges are sanded to reduce the potential for bruises if the cheerleader slips and lands on the edge of the base.
- To assemble, screw the nipple into the base, and then the step on the other end.

Description:

- The top person/flyer starts with her right foot on the top of the pedestal.
- The top person/flyer steps upon the pedestal balancing on one leg.
- The top person/flyer locks out her knee and squares her shoulders and hips over her foot.
- Her arms immediately hit a high-V position.
- The top person/flyer balances in this position for 10 seconds.
- The top person/flyer repeats the drill on her left leg.
- The top person/flyer completes five sets.

Coaching Points:

- Using a cheer pedestal is an excellent balance-training tool to teach the proper technique and positions for a top person/flyer at a low risk level.
- Stepping up on a pedestal activates the muscles to tighten in order to stay on the small platform.
- This challenge gives the top person/flyer the feel of the stunt so she will have more confident to execute the stunt at a higher height.
- The top person/flyer must not lean or dip her shoulders or hips as she steps up on the pedestal.
- The top person/flyer should look out and up while she is on the pedestal not down at her foot or the floor. Looking down transfers her balance point and will cause her to fall out of a stunt.

- The top person/flyer needs to lift her toes upward in her shoes to avoid pointing her toes downward. This downward process is referred to as "toeing" in the cheerleading world.
- Search the Internet for the many varieties of cheer pedestals: Pro-Pedestal®, Stunt Pedestal®, Twist and Shout Pedestal®, and Cheerleading Stunt Stand®.

Variations:
- The top person/flyer performs the same drill, hitting the following positions at the top: heel stretch, arabesque, scorpion, scale, and bow and arrow.

Variation—heel stretch

#77: Standing Balance Board Progressions

Objective: To increase core strength and stability and improve the cheerleader's sense of proprioception for the top person/flyer

Equipment Needed: Balance board, a mat

Description:
- Place the board on a matted surface beside a wall.
- The cheerleader begins with both feet apart on the balance board. She progresses through the following sequence; doing each step for one minute.
    - ✓ Step One: She rocks the board forward and backward, then side to side, continuing this process until she has total control of the board.
    - ✓ Step Two: She rotates the board around with its edges, making contact to the floor.
    - ✓ Step Three: She balances on the board without letting its edges touch the floor.
    - ✓ Step Four: She balances on the board with her eyes closed.
    - ✓ Step Five: She balances on the board while performing the following skills on one leg: liberty, scorpion, scale, arabesque, and heel stretch positions.

Coaching Points:
- The one-leg balancing exercises simulate the skills the top person/flyer must executes when elevated in a one-legged stunt.
- Several types of balance boards, also called wobble boards or rocker boards, are available on the market. They vary in size and material. Look for them on the Internet.
- To make one, cut a croquet ball in half and secure a round, flat wooden circle on the cut side of the ball.
- These drills also strengthen and increase the ankle's range of motion.
- The board can also be used for rehabilitation of the ankle. The cheerleader sits in a chair with both feet on the board. She moves it in a circle with her feet.

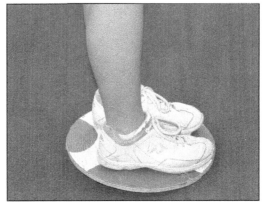
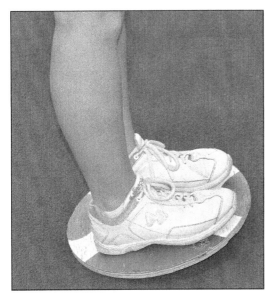
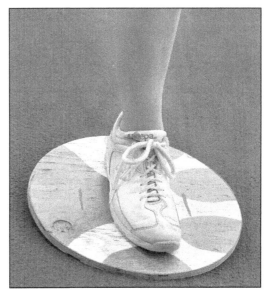

#78: Hang Practice

Objective: To teach the proper load-in position for the top person/flyer

Equipment Needed: Matted surface

Description:
- Needed is one stunt group: a top person/flyer, two bases, and a back spotter.
- The top person/flyer places her hands on the shoulders of the bases.
- The back spotter grabs hold of the top person/flyer's waist as the she bends her knees and jumps upward and locks out her arms.
- The top person/flyer tucks in her knees to her chest.
- At this point, the back spotter releases the top person/flyer's waist.
- The top person/flyer holds her pose for 10 seconds.
- The top person/flyer carefully returns her feet to the floor and her arms to her side.
- Once the top person/flyer masters the proper body position, line up several rows of bases and have the top person/flyer do 30-second hang drills with each set of bases as she progresses down the row.

Coaching Points:
- This sport-specific drill teaches the top person/flyer to use her stomach muscles to maintain the proper tucked body position and her arms to hold her own body weight when loading into a stunt.
- The bases need to stand the top person/flyer's shoulder-width apart in order for the top person/flyer to have her arms directly under her body.

Variation:
- Use two chairs for this drill in place of the bases.
- Have your top person/flyer squat on the floor between the two chairs. She will then put her hands on the seat of the chairs and lift herself up, locking out her arms and pulling her knees to her chest.

#79: Pop Cradling Position

Objective: To learn proper body position for the top person/flyer while she is in the air during the toss portion of a cradle

Equipment Needed: Matted surface

Description:
- The top person/flyer lies on her back on the floor with her feet apart and her arms over her head in a high-V position.
- On designated count, the top person/flyer pulls her legs together and snaps her arms to her side as she tightens her body, arches her back, and points her toes.
- The top person/flyer does this 20 times.

Coaching Points:
- This drill enforces not only the correct body position, but helps the cheerleader understand timing and body awareness.
- Doing these movements while lying on the floor helps the top person/flyer to perfect her cradling technique in a safe, low-risk environment.
- While cradling, a top person/flyer tends to drop her shoulders back and fall out of the cradle. This drill reinforces the concept that she needs to pull her torso up (not back) when tossed.

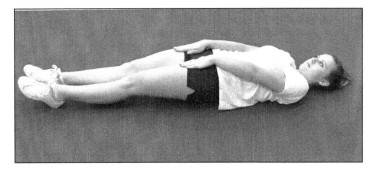

#80: Disc Twist

Objective: To perfect proper technique in twisting for full down cradles

Equipment Needed: Frisbee®

Description:
- Place the Frisbee upside-down on the floor.
- The top person/flyer stands behind the Frisbee with her feet together and her arms in a high-V position.
- The top person/flyer steps onto the Frisbee with one foot as she place the other foot tight to the stepping foot.
- The top person/flyer immediately looks over her left shoulder as she pulls her arms diagonally down to her side like she is putting her left hand in a back pocket and her right hand in her left pocket.
- Her whole body turns around one time.
- The top person/flyer stops the spin by stepping off the Frisbee after one rotation.
- The top person/flyer spots with her eyes to the front in order to attain a constant orientation.
- The top person/flyer repeats this drill 10 times.

Coaching Points:
- The cheerleader should not lean or pull her body out of alignment. She stays straight and tight as a pole during this drill.
- In a full-down cradle, a cheerleader tends to throw her body, leaning with her right shoulder in order to twist one rotation. This reaction causes her to move out of alignment with the bases, which makes her hard to catch.
- The cheerleader learns from this drill that looking first with her head and pulling only with the arms will keep her centered over the bases and still able to easily complete the rotation. The cheerleader's gaze is on a single location at the front of the stunt.

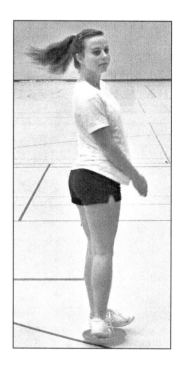

Variations:
- Repeat the same drill, but the cheerleader places only one foot on the Frisbee and then spins.
- Have the cheerleader spin around two times before stepping off the Frisbee.

#81: Log Roll

Objective: To develop proper twisting technique for the top person/flyer

Equipment Needed: Matted surface

Description:
- The cheerleader, with her arms by her side, starts in a cradle position in the arms of two bases with a back spotter.
- The group, on a designated count, dips through their legs and pops the top person/flyer into the air.
- The top person/flyer stays horizontal and initiates barrel roll-type twist to her left by looking to her left.
- The base group catches the top person/flyer in a cradle.
- The group repeats the drill five times.

Coaching Points:
- The initial attempts may result in the top person/flyer landing on her side or stomach.
- The top person/flyer needs to wait for the pop before she begins to twist; otherwise, she will rotate against the bases' arms and out of the group.
- The top person/flyer spots to the front, focusing her eyes on one object. During the twist, she rotates looking from that spot around to the left and back to the spot. This concept helps her body fully rotate around.
- A tight body position of the top person/flyer will assist in the completion of the twist.

Basing and Spotting Drills

Practicing sport-specific drills by focusing on a particular player helps each team member understand and execute their part while stunting. The following skills and drills are aimed at the cheerleaders that do the lifting and spotting of the top person/flyer. Timing and strength are the two key elements that need to be perfected in order to build safe and sturdy stunts.

#82: Shoe Practice

Objective: To teach proper hand placement for the bases while stunting

Equipment Needed: Pair of shoes

Description:
- The base grips the bottom of a tennis shoe by placing her palm under the heel and wrapping the fingers around the side of the shoe. The other palm of the hand is under the toe and the fingers are wrapped around the side of the shoe.
- The base cups the shoe close to her body with her elbows tucked into her side.
- The base simulates the steps of a load-in position to a prep position.
- As she moves the shoe to just below her chin, the base rotates the palms of the hands under the center of the shoe and her fingertips grip around the edge of the toe and heel area.
- Her elbows and forearms come together, squeezing tightly in front of her chest.

Coaching Tips:
- Bases often tend to rotate their hands too far outward on the top person/flyer's shoe, keeping only the heel of the hand under the toe and heel areas of the shoe and leaving a gap under the center of the shoe. Doing so causes the top person/flyer to rock back and forth in the stunt because she does not have a firm platform to stand on.
- The base must understand to rotate the heels of her palms together to make a solid platform for the top person/flyer.
- Proper hand position is key to building a solid foundation for the top person/flyer in order for her to execute advanced stunts. With a flat, squared, hand platform under the top person/flyer's shoes, the top person/flyer will be able to maintain a squared, balanced body in fully extended two-legged and one-legged stunts.

#83: Base Timing

Objective: To synchronize the bases' timing and technique

Equipment Needed: None

Description:
- Three people are needed: two bases and a back spotter.
- The bases set up in the starting position for building a stunt. Their feet are apart; their hands are cupped together and pulled close to their mid-section with elbows squeezing their sides.
- The bases stand facing each other and about a foot apart.
- While the bases walk through the building of a prep, the back spotter pushes down on the bases' hands with her hands, imitating the weight of a top person/flyer loading into a stunt.
- They perform this drill five times.

Coaching Points:
- Check to ensure that the bases are bending their knees at the same time and depth as they walk through the dip in the building process.
- The back spotter can feel if the bases are lifting their hands from the start position to the shoulders at the same time and speed. Have her explain to the bases whose timing is off.
- Work this drill until both bases have the same timing, placement, and speed.
- This is a low-risk drill that brings timing and body awareness to the bases in order to perform a safe and well-executed prep when a top person/flyer is in it.

#84: Stunt Squat Practice

Objective: To synchronize the bases in the depth of their dip; to teach them the concept of using their legs when building and cradling stunts

Equipment Needed: Matted surface

Description:

- The stunt group (two bases, top person/flyer, back spotter) builds a prep/elevator.
- The back spotter holds onto the back of the top person/flyer's thighs for safety.
- The spotter focuses her attention on the head, neck, and shoulders of the top person/flyer in preparation to catch her if she falls out of the stunt.
- The back spotter calls the eight-count sequence for the bases to dip. She yells, "Five, six, seven, eight," and on count one, two, the bases dip through their legs, and on count three, four the bases straighten their legs; on count five, six, they dip again and straighten on count seven, eight.
- The top person/flyer keeps her body tight from head to toe and her arms placed in a high-V as the bases move up and down.
- One eight-count equals a set.
- The group completes 10 sets.

Coaching Points:

- Bases have a tendency to only shrug from their shoulders instead of using the power in their legs when stunting. Doing this drill helps them develop proper technique, timing, and body awareness.
- Often as stunt groups get comfortable with building, they tend to fall back to old habits. Doing this drill daily reinforces the value of strong leg muscles and proper technique, which, in turn, develops muscle memory.
- Also this drill teaches the top person/flyer the importance of a tight, squared body needed for balance.

#85: The Water Glass

Objective: To assist the base in learning proper hand position when performing a full up extension

Equipment Needed: Plastic glass filled halfway with water

Description:
- The base grasps under the water glass with her right hand. Her elbow faces away from her body.
- The base places her hand with the water glass close to her stomach/belly bottom area and puts her left hand under her right hand.
- Her feet are apart and both knees are bent.
- On a designated count, the base dips lower through her knees. At the same time, she rotates her right hand up and around to her right as she pulls her elbow in toward her body.
- Maintaining a flat surface with her right hand, the base twist the glass 360 degrees around and up over her head.
- At the top, the base pretends to grab the heel of the shoe with her left hand.

Coaching Points:
- This drill reinforces the need for the base to keep the water glass (shoe) flat while twisting a top person/flyer to the top. Often, the downward weight of the cheerleader causes the base to pull her hand out to the front of her body, resulting in the cheerleader spinning away from the stunt group.
- Due to the awkward twist on the base's right hand and arm, it is essential that the base grabs the heel of the shoe quickly with her left hand.
- This drill can also be done with the water glass placed in the top person/flyer's right shoe.

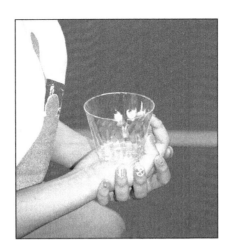

> **Stunt Group Drills**
>
> Cheerleading is a team sport made of a bunch of smaller teams or stunts. Working together is key to success. In order to develop timing, trust, and proper technique, the groups need to practice as a unit. Following are some drills that reinforce the needed skills.

#86: Stunt Circuit

Objective: To develop strength, coordination, proper technique, team unity, and synchronization

Equipment Needed: Open gym space

Description:
- In single file, line your cheerleaders up in groups of four: top person/flyer, right base, left base, and back spotter.
- Place groups a straight line, approximately two feet apart.
- Using an eight-count, each top person/flyer jumps into a load-in position into the hands of a stunt group on counts one, two, three, four, holds in the load-in position for counts five, six, seven, eight, then dismounts.
- Have each top person/flyer change groups by moving down the line by one group.
- Perform another sequence of loads and dismounts using two sets of eight-counts: one set to do the stunt and one set to move to the next stunt group.
- They continue to do this series until the top persons/flyers have returned to their original group.
- They repeat the entire rotation, but this time the right bases cycle through each stunt group.
- They repeat the entire rotation, but this time the left bases cycle through each stunt group.
- They repeat the entire rotation, but this time the back spotters cycle through each stunt group.

Coaching Points:
- This is a great drill to use at the beginning of the season.
- Every group has a slightly different timing and, at first, each group will lack synchronization and coordination when a new person is substituted. About halfway through the entire sequence, you should begin to see improvement.
- The opportunity for each cheerleader to work in several groups will increase the overall versatility of the team.
- This is also an overall conditioning drill, working the major muscle groups from legs, to arms, to core.

#87: Earthquake

Objective: To reinforce trust within the stunt group and a tight body for the top person/flyer

Equipment Needed: Matted floor

Description:
- A stunt group consisting of two bases, a back spotter, and a top person/flyer build a prep/elevator.
- The bases move their hands and knees, shaking the top person/flyer like she is in an earthquake.
- The back spotter holds onto the top person/flyer's thighs and watches the top person/flyer in case she falls.
- The top person/flyer should try to not fall by keeping her body square and tight as a board as she is being shaken.
- The top person/flyer looks out and up, not down at the floor or the bases during the shaking.
- The stunt group performs the sequence for 10 seconds. They do five sets.

Coaching Points:
- The idea of this drill is to teach the top person/flyer to stay tight when the bases are moving and not fall out of the stunt. Often, a top person/flyer will give up, relax her body, and fall out of a stunt. This reaction is called "bailing" in cheerleading language.
- If the top person/flyer does not maintain a locked, straight body, the bases cannot keep her up over their heads in the air. It is like the difference between trying to balance a board or a rubber hose in the air.

#88: Retake

Objective: To develop proper technique, control, and timing in building a prep/elevator or full extension

Equipment Needed: A matted floor

Description:
- This drill needs a stunt group consisting of a top person/flyer, two bases, and a back spotter.
- The group builds a prep/elevator.
- Next, the stunt group retakes the top person/flyer to the load-in position.
- Bases hands come down to their belly buttons as they continue to hold onto the top person/flyer's feet.
- The top person/flyer grabs the bases' shoulders, keeping her arms locked out straight and supporting her weight in her arms.
- The top person/flyer pulls her knees to her chest, keeping her chest up and feet flat in the bases' hands.
- The back spotter maintains contact with the top person/flyer's ankles as she watches the head, neck, and shoulders of the top person/flyer.
- The bases and back spotter, then, take the top person/flyer back up to a prep/elevator as the top person/flyer locks out her knees and pulls her body up to a standing position.
- Repeat this sequence five times in a row, working their way up to 10 reps.

Coaching Points:
- Check that the top person/flyer does not sit back into the load-in position. She should have her shoulders, hips, and feet in alignment.
- Check that the top person/flyer catches herself with her arms on the shoulders of the bases. She should not bend her elbows during the downward movements.

- Watch the timing to assure that the top person/flyer stands at the same instant as the bases stand up when they are retaking her back to the prep/elevator. Often, the top person/flyer will stand up too soon, causing her to push the bases' hands downward as they are trying to lift her.
- The top person/flyer needs to contract her inner thighs as she stands and rides up into the prep/elevator. Often, the top person/flyer will push her legs outward, causing the bases to step back out of the stunt.
- Make sure that the bases keep their backs straight and bend from their knees when retaking the top person/flyer to the load-in position.
- Verify that the back spotter keeps contact with the top person/flyer's ankles and does not let the top person/flyer sit into her hands.

#89: Show and Go

Objective: To develop key muscles for stunting; to perfect technique; to work timing

Equipment Needed: Matted surface

Description:
- This drill needs a stunt group with a top person/flyer, two bases, and a back spotter.
- The top person/flyer loads into the hands of the bases with the assistance of the back spotter.
- The bases grab the top person/flyer's feet and immediately lift her straight up overhead, fully extending their arms as the top person/flyer pulls up through her shoulders to a straight body position, with arms in a high-V.
- The bases must propel the top person/flyer upward, using the power from their legs.
- The back spotter will grabs the top person/flyer's ankles on the way up, helping to fully extend her over the heads of the bases.
- The bases do not stop the stunt at the top, but return the top person/flyer back to the load-in position.
- As the top person/flyer returns to the load-in position, the bases absorb the downward momentum through their legs and arms, making sure not to lean forward from their waist.
- Repeat series 10 times.

Coaching Points:
- Reinforce the need for the bases to pull their elbows into their bodies during the load-in position, bending their knees and keeping their backs straight.
- If the stunt gets stuck part way up and the bases have a hard time completely extending their arms, it is because the bases are not using their legs to propel the top person/flyer upward.

- Check to see that the bases' backs are straight and not arched when their arms are fully extended. Arching their back could cause injury to the lower back.
- It is important that the bases learn to resist the downward momentum by tightening their muscles as the top person/flyer comes down. Often, bases relax through their arms and legs, causing the top person/flyer to come down too quickly, resulting in possible injury to both the bases and top person/flyer.
- In order to stop the top person/flyer on the downward move, the bases tend to lean forward at the waist. Injury could occur due to improper body alignment. Also, the bases could hit their heads together if they lean inward.
- The bases also tend to drop their hands below their waists at the bottom of the downward movement, which could cause injury to their wrists.
- Not only is this drill an excellent exercise in developing strength, timing, and proper technique, it is also a skill used in transitional stunting.

#90: Assisted Twist Cradle

Objective: To learn how to do twisting full down cradles

Equipment Needed: Matted surface

Description:
- Five cheerleaders are needed for this skill: top person/flyer, two bases, back spotter, and front spotter.
- The top person/flyer starts in an elevator/prep stunt in the hands of two bases with a back spotter.
- A front spotter faces the stunt. She crosses her right arm over her left arm. She grabs the top person/flyer's right ankle with her right hand. She grabs the top person/flyer's left ankle with her left hand.
- On a designated count from the back spotter, the bases dip together and propel the top person/flyer into the air. The front spotter maintains contact with the top person/flyer's ankles.
- The top person/flyer pulls her body upward and twists one rotation to her left, keeping her body straight.
- The front spotter assists the top person/flyer's rotation by bringing her right arm across and around as her left hand twist to the left. She does not let go of the top person/flyer's ankles.

Coaching Points:
- Spotting to the front while twisting is key for the top person/flyer in order to stay centered over the bases. It provides a fixed focal point for the eyes. She must look over her left shoulder and to the front as she rotates; not down to the ground or at the back spotter. A rule for her to remember is the head leads the body.
- Check that the top person/flyer does not jump out of the bases' hands; she must wait for them to toss her in the air.
- The top person/flyer must travel upward and rotates at the top of the toss. Often, a cheerleader twists before hitting the top of the toss, causing her to throw herself out of alignment and to come down crooked. Having a person on her ankles helps keep her in proper alignment with her stunt group.
- Repeat the assisted drill until the top person/flyer is able to do the twist properly by herself.

#91: Toss Practice

Objective: To develop trust and proper body position for the top person/flyer; to strengthen leg and arm muscles of the bases

Equipment Needed: Matted surface

Description:
- The top person/flyer begins in a cradle position in the arms of two bases and a back spotter.
- The bases and back spotter toss the top person/flyer straight upward into the air. Bases propel her upward using their legs and extending their arms as high as possible.
- The top person/flyer remains tight with her legs squeezed together, arms in a T-position while airborne and through the return to the cradle position.
- On the re-catch, the bases must capture the top person/flyer as high as possible in the air and resist the downward movement by absorbing her body weight through their legs.

Coaching Points:
- In order to increase safety and trust, the top person/flyer, bases, and back spotter must work together as one synchronized unit with each person executing the proper technique for their position.
- This low-risk drill creates trust between the bases and the top person/flyer.
- During the toss drill focus on the bases' form; check that they both bend their knees to the same depth, creating equal force on the upward lift through the legs.
- It is key when the bases toss the cheerleader into the air that their arms stay extended and ready to catch the top person/flyer as she comes down. Often, bases bring their arms back to their chest/waist area and wait for the cheerleader to come down to them. This improper form of catching too low results in the possibility that the top person/flyer's back could hit the bases/back spotter's knees.

#92: Liberty Progression

Objective: To progressively train a liberty that is directly in line with the group's skill level

Equipment Needed: Matted surface, a chair

Description:

- Step 1: Using a standard chair, the top person/flyer uses two eight-counts to execute this load-in sequence for a liberty.
    - ✓ The top person/flyer starts with her right foot on the center of the chair, and arms by her side.
    - ✓ The top person/flyer begins counting with five, six, seven, eight, and she bends her left knee on count one, two.
    - ✓ The top person/flyer jumps off the left leg on count three, four and stands up on her right leg that is on the chair as she extends her arms to a high-V.
    - ✓ The top person/flyer holds the position on the chair for five, six, seven, eight.
    - ✓ The top person/flyer steps back to the floor on her left leg, bringing her arms back to her side on count one, two.
    - ✓ The top person/flyer holds that position for count three, four, five, six, seven, eight.
    - ✓ Once the top person/flyer has mastered this step with proper technique and balance, she moves on to the next step.
- Step 2: This step needs three more cheerleaders. They form a stunt group of two bases and a back spotter.
    - ✓ The top person/flyer places her right foot into the hands of the two bases, using a liberty grip.
    - ✓ The group is the replacement for the chair. They hold their position with their knees bent as the top person/flyer steps up on to the bases' hands, using the same counts as in Step 1.
    - ✓ After the top person/flyer has perfected this series, the group moves to the next step.
- Step 3: The group synchronizes the series with the top person/flyer while lifting her to their navel level and returning her to the floor.
    - ✓ They begin counting with five, six, seven, eight.
    - ✓ The group dips on count one, two.
    - ✓ The group stands, straightening their legs, and lifts the top person/flyer to their navel level on count three, four.

- ✓ They hold the top person/flyer at this position for counts five, six, seven, eight.
- ✓ They return to the starting position by bending their knees and with the top person/flyer's left foot back on the floor on count one, two, three, four.
- ✓ The group works through the sequence until properly executed.
- Step 4: Using the same counts as in Step 3, the group lifts the top person/flyer to their chest level and returns her to the starting position.
  - ✓ Once they have perfected this step, they advance to the next step.
- Step 5: The group lifts the top person/flyer to a fully extended position over the bases' head with the assistance of the back spotter, and then returns her to the starting position.
  - ✓ The group dips on count one, two; lifts the top person/flyer fully extended over their heads on three, four, five, six, and immediately brings her back down to the floor on counts seven, eight.
  - ✓ The top person/flyer remains tight throughout the entire sequence. She does not bend her right leg until count seven in order to place her left foot on the floor.
  - ✓ After the group has perfected this step, they move to the final step.
- Step 6: Using the first half of counts, the group will perform the drill that ends in a liberty.
  - ✓ The count begins with count five, six, seven, eight.
  - ✓ The group dips on count one, two.
  - ✓ The top person/flyer pushes off the floor with her left foot on count three and stands up on her right leg on count four.
  - ✓ The group drives the top person/flyer up on three, four, five, six.
  - ✓ They stop at the top and hold top person/flyer in the overhead position.
  - ✓ She pulls her left foot to her left knee and her arms hit a high-V.
  - ✓ To dismount, they slowly (and in a controlled manner) return her to the starting position.

Coaching Points:
- This progression drill takes several practices to perfect.
- Each stunt group needs to perfect each individual step before moving on to the next step.
- In Steps 2 through 6, the top person/flyer places her hands on the bases' shoulders as she returns her left foot to the floor. She supports her body weight on their shoulders in order to not slam her foot into the floor.
- For safety, surround the stunt with four corner spotting during Steps 4 through 6.

#93: Partner Stunt Floor Liberty

Objective: To learn proper hand technique for co-ed partner liberty stunt; to perfect balance for the top person/flyer

Equipment Needed: Matted surface

Description:
- Four cheerleaders are needed for this drill: a base, a top person/flyer, and two spotters.
- The base lies on his back on the floor with his arms extended up toward the ceiling.
- The base flexes his hands placing his left hand in front of his right.
- Place an extra person on both sides of the base to safety spot the top person/flyer when she steps into the base's hands.
- The top person/flyer, standing behind the base's head, steps up on the extended hands of the base and balances on her right leg. She places her left foot beside her right knee and her arms extend in a T-position.
- The base grips the heel of the shoe with his right hand and the ball of the foot with his left hand.
- The base locks out his arms and shoulders.
- The top person/flyer balances with her arms in a high-V position without the assistance of the spotters.
- The two cheerleaders maintain this position for 30 seconds.
- The top person/flyer steps back out of the stunt with her left foot. The extra person assists in the dismount, assuring that the top person/flyer steps away from the base lying on the floor.
- The cheerleaders repeat the sequence five times.

Coaching Points:
- This drill helps the base get the feel for alignment of hands and the proper grip on the top person/flyer's shoe. Check that the base's hands grip the entire shoes. The base tightens through the shoulders and arms.
- The top person/flyer needs to square her body directly over the base's hands by pulling up through her body. Check to see that her hips and shoulders are square to the front.
- This low-risk drill helps both cheerleaders perfect their technique so they properly execute an extended coed-based liberty.

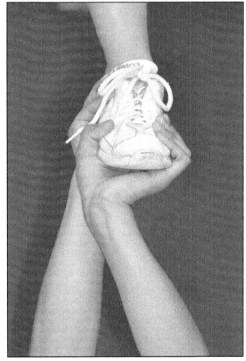

#94: Coed Toss Drill

Objective: To develop timing and proper technique for coed partner stunting

Equipment Needed: Matted surface

Description:
- The top person/flyer stands in front of the primary base. Both athletes face forward.
- The base stands with his feet apart, placing his right foot slightly in front of his left.
- The base grabs the waist of the top person/flyer.
- The top person/flyer stands with her feet together and hands gripping the base's wrists.
- On count one, two, both the top person/flyer and the base bend their knees. This bending is also called a "dip."
- On count three, four, the base explodes through his arms and legs, lifting the top person/flyer off the floor. At the same time, she jumps as high as she can and pulls up through her shoulders.
- At the top of the lift, the base follows through with his hands by straightening his arms and wrists and flicking the cheerleader high into the air.
- The top person/flyer at the top of the toss flicks downward with her wrists and straightens her arms to get more height during the toss.
- The base keeps his arms extended and catches the top person/flyer at her waist on the way down from the toss.
- He absorbs the catch through his legs in order to slow the downward movement of the cheerleader.
- The top person/flyer regrabs the base's wrists, catching her body weight in both her arms and legs as she reaches the floor.
- The cheerleaders repeat this drill five times. They do three sets with a rest period in between sets.

Coaching Points:
- The base must wait for the top person/flyer's upward explosion to lift the girl into the air. Too often, the base grips the top person/flyer's waist too tightly and pulls downward on the cheerleader during the dip, causing her to not be able to explode off the floor with her legs.
- The base must fully extend his arms and then flick at the top as he tosses the cheerleader into the air. Often, the base tries to toss the girl when his arms are bent, causing the cheerleader to not get enough height.

- During the flicking process, check that the base's thumbs are facing upward at the end of the toss.
- Check the timing of the base to see that his arms hit their full extension at the same time as his legs are fully straight from the bend.
- Have the base add an explosive hop with his legs at the top of the toss.
- The base needs to toss the cheerleader upward, not forward.
- As the top person/flyer dips, her elbows are pointing backward toward the base, not lifted out to the side.
- The top person/flyer jumps off the floor slightly backward into the base.
- The top person/flyer should keep her feet together on the way up and down.
- The top person/flyer should flick her arms down her body. Check to see that she is not pushing her arms out and away from her body as she flicks off the wrists of the base.
- Timing is key to executing this drill. Both the top person/flyer and the base must flick at the same time waiting until the very top of the toss.

#95: Trophy Stance

Objective: To perfect the beginning steps for a basket toss

Equipment Needed: Matted surface

Description:
- This drill needs a stunt group with a top person/flyer, two bases, and a back spotter.
- Bases interlace their hands in a basket toss grip.
- The top person/flyer jumps into their hands with assistance from the back spotter.
- The top person/flyer places the ball of her feet on the forward part of the bases' interlaced hands. Her knees are bent, and her hands are on the bases' shoulders.
- The bases lift the top person/flyer upward as she stands. Her feet do not leave the hands of the bases.
- The bases stall slightly at the top and hold her like she is a trophy.
- Next, the stunt group returns to the beginning position, where the top person/flyer bends her knees and her hands come down to the bases' shoulders.
- The group performs 10 repetitions.

Coaching Points:
- It is important to have spotters positioned around the stunt for safety when first learning this drill.
- The top person/flyer, keeping her body tight, straight, and squared, needs to balance on the hands of the bases as she stands at the very top of the stunt.
- This drill teaches the top person/flyer that during a basket toss, she must only stand straight up, not jump upward during a basket toss. Jumping will cause the top person/flyer to go forward or backward out of the hands of the stunt group.
- It is easier for the bases to control the top person/flyer if she concentrates on the straight body alignment and lets the bases throw her in the air to get the height during a basket toss.

FLEXIBILITY DRILLS

Flexibility is often only associated with the top persons/flyers because they hit heel stretches, scales, and scorpion positions when in the air. Cheerleading stunts require extensive flexibility in both the lifting and tossing done by the bases/spotters and the stretch and skills performed at the top of the stunt by the top persons/flyers. Flexibility creates better form and prevents injuries by increasing range of motion through the joints. Not only are stretch drills needed to be done at the gym during practices, but should be supplemented with stretching exercises at home.

#96: Inch Worm

Objective: To warm up the total body in order to prepare it to take on the challenging moves and positions in cheerleading

Equipment Needed: None

Description:
- The cheerleader, from a standing position, leans her body forward from her waist and places her hands on the floor to stabilize her spine.
- Next, the cheerleader slowly drops her hips to the floor as she stretches the front torso forward, walking her hands away from her feet. Her heels will rise off the floor. The cheerleader should try to keep the knees straight.
- Her body will extend out parallel to the floor in a plank position with hands directly under the shoulders. Her head is aligned with the spine.
- Next, the cheerleader slowly walks her feet to her hands. She keeps her hands planted on the floor.
- Lastly, the cheerleader walks her hand forward again, keeping the feet stationary, extending her body out to a plank position.
- Have the cheerleader repeat this sequence five times, and challenge the cheerleaders to work up to 10 times.

Coaching Points:
- This drill is a good all-over stretch and workout using the muscles needed for stunting.
- To prevent injury to the back during this drill, the cheerleader needs to keep her back straight and muscles engaged throughout the movement, especially when body is stretched out in a plank position. Do not let her arch the back or sag in the middle while in the plank position.
- The cheerleader should not reach too far forward when leaning down from the standing position because it will put too much stress on the shoulders.
- The plank position is very effective in strengthening the upper body.
- Divide the cheerleaders into two equal groups. Challenge the cheerleaders to do this drill one at a time across the gym floor and back. The first team to have all their cheerleaders finish is declared the winner.

#97: Chair Leg Lifts

Objective: To develop top person/flyer's quadriceps and hamstring strength and flexibility

Equipment Needed: Chair

Description:
- The cheerleader stands tall with her arms in a T-position, facing away from the chair approximately a leg length.
- The cheerleader places her right foot on the chair with her toes pointed and her leg straight.
- Standing tall, the cheerleader slowly lifts her back leg up and down without it touching the chair.
- The cheerleader performs this move 10 times.
- The cheerleader changes to her left leg and repeats lifting the extended back leg 10 times.
- Ten lifts on each leg is one set.
- The cheerleader completes three sets.

Coaching Points:
- Check the cheerleader's posture. Don't let her lean forward in order to lift the leg higher.
- The cheerleader does not bend the knee during the lifting. The power is centered in the buttock, quadriceps, and hamstrings.
- This sport-specific drill helps increase the range of motion through the top person/flyer's legs and back.
- To increase difficulty, add a small folded mat on the chair. Adding more height, will increase the cheerleader's flexibility.
- In stunting, a top person/flyer is extended in the air on one foot and then must hit different positions like a heel stretch and an arabesque. If a cheerleader cannot

stretch her leg straight and close to her body when doing heel stretches, it is because she lacks the needed strength and elasticity. It is essential that she works these key elements of strength and flexibility for proper form. Too often cheerleaders only concentrate on balance. With lack of leg power, the cheerleader dangles her leg too low when demonstrating complex skills like arabesques.

Variation:
- The cheerleader starts facing the chair.
- The cheerleader extends her right leg in front of her and puts her foot on the chair.
- With a lifted torso, the cheerleader elevates her leg up and down 10 times, not letting her foot touch the chair.
- The cheerleader repeats the drill with her left leg.
- The cheerleader does three sets.

#98: Top Person/Flyer Stretches

Objective: To work stability and increase flexibility in the hip flexors

Equipment Needed: Resistance bands

Description:
- This is a two-part drill. First, the cheerleader must work on balance, and once mastered, she then proceeds on to increasing her flexibility.
- The cheerleader has the center of the band wrapped once around the ankle of her left leg. The ends of the band are in both hands.
- Balancing on her right leg, the cheerleader lifts the left leg straight out behind her in an arabesque.
- Pulling the end of the bands out with her arms in a T-position, the cheerleader brings the leg up as high as possible and holds for a count of 30.
- Next, the cheerleader brings her hands over her head and pulls the extended leg up into a scale position and holds for 30 seconds.
- The cheerleader reverses to the other leg and repeats the set.

Coaching Points:
- Often, cheerleaders have better balance and are more flexible on one dominant side. They will want to work only that leg, believing that they cannot and are not able to increase their flexibility on the weaker side. Always have them work both legs when stretching. In time, they will see that flexibility and balance can be achieved on both legs.
- When building pyramids, top person/flyers need the capability to balance on either the right or left leg. Developing this skill will make the team able to execute elite-level stunting.

Variation—Scorpion:
- A cheerleader wraps the center of the band around her left ankle.
- Balancing on her right leg, the cheerleader lifts the left leg up behind her, bending her knee this time and pulling on the ends of the band as she extends her arms over her head.
- The cheerleader holds that scorpion position for a count of eight.
- Next, the cheerleader pulls the leg closer to her head by shortening the distance between the hands on the band and the ankle.
- The cheerleader holds for a second count of eight.
- The cheerleader carefully lowers her leg back to the ground.
- The cheerleader reverses legs and repeats drill on the right leg.

Variation—Scorpion

#99: Wall Stretches

Objective: To develop flexibility in hips, legs, and back of the top person/flyer

Equipment Needed: Unobstructed wall area

Description:
- Two cheerleaders are needed to execute this drill.
- The top person/flyer, facing the wall, places both hands on the wall while she lifts her right leg straight behind her.
- Her partner places the top person/flyer's ankle on her right shoulder and grabs under the top person/flyer's right thigh with her left hand.
- Next, the partner exerts gentle pressure upward on the top person/flyer's leg for 30 seconds.
- They rest and repeat the drill on the opposite leg.
- The group does three sets of 30 seconds on each leg

Coaching Points:
- Check the top person/flyer for proper body alignment with squared hips and shoulders.
- Reinforce the need for the cheerleader to have pointed toes and eyes looking forward or upward.
- Developing flexibility through the hips, shoulders, legs, and back is a slow process and should not be forced.
- Doing these drills on a daily bases will greatly increase the top person/flyer's flexibility.

Variations:
- Scorpion
    - ✓ Repeat the same drill except this time the second cheerleader bends the top person/flyer's leg into a scorpion position.
    - ✓ The top person/flyer grabs her foot, if possible.
    - ✓ The partner cheerleader exerts gentle pressure under the thigh of the cheerleader in the scorpion position.
    - ✓ The group does three sets of 30 seconds on each leg.
- Heel Stretch
    - ✓ The top person/flyer has her back to the wall and extends her leg straight up to the front.
    - ✓ The partner grabs the calf and heel of the extended leg and applies pressure upward.
    - ✓ They hold this position for 30 seconds.
    - ✓ The cheerleader repeats the drill with the other leg.
    - ✓ The group does three sets of 30 seconds on each leg.

- Bow and Arrow
  - ✓ The top person/flyer stand with her right shoulder toward the wall.
  - ✓ She extends her left leg straight up into the air beside her left shoulder. She places her right arm across her body.
  - ✓ The partner presses the left leg up with her right hand on the top person/flyer's heel and pulls the top person/flyer's left arm across her body in a T-position.
  - ✓ They maintain this pose for 30 seconds.
  - ✓ The group does three sets of 30 seconds on each leg.

Variation—Scorpion

Variation—Heel Stretch

Variation—Bow and Arrow

#100: Kneeling Heel Stretch

Objective: To develop flexibility and range of motion in the hips

Equipment Needed: Matted surface

Description:
- Two people are needed for this drill.
- One cheerleader kneels in front of and facing away from the second cheerleader.
- The front cheerleader wraps her arms around the back person's legs.
- The front cheerleader extends her right leg up in front of her as the back person grabs her ankle.
- Pulling gently on the leg, the back person holds the front cheerleader's leg for 30 seconds.
- Have the floor cheerleader reverse legs and repeat.
- The group does three sets of 30 seconds on each leg.

#101: Partner Arm Stretch

Objective: To develop flexibility and range of motion in the shoulders for the bases

Equipment Needed: None

Description:
- Two people are needed for this drill.
- One cheerleader stands in front of the other.
- The front person extends her arms straight behind her.
- The cheerleader in the back grabs the front cheerleader's arms just above the elbows and pulls them together and upward.
- They hold this position for 30 seconds.
- Have the cheerleaders repeat this sequence five times.
- The cheerleaders switch positions and repeat the drill.

Coaching Points:
- Because the shoulder muscles are constantly being used in both stunting and tumbling, stretching improves their range of motion.
- This is a good drill to use both as a warm-up before the cheerleaders start stunting and as a cool-down afterward.
- This stretch relieves tension through the shoulders and alleviates pain.
- As with any stretch, it should be done slowly. The partner gently exerts pressure on the arms.

About the Authors

Pam Headridge has participated in a wide variety of cheerleading in her 24-year career, including coach, judge, competition director, state tournament manager, national speaker, and author.

She has been honored as National Cheerleading Coach of the Year, *American Cheerleader* magazine's Outstanding High School Coach of the Year, Washington State Cheerleading Coaches Association Hall of Fame, Cheer Ltd Pinnacle of Excellence Award, PacWest Lifetime Achievement Award, and National Federation of High School National Coach.

Headridge has published two other books: *Developing a Successful Cheerleading Program*, and *101 School Spirit Ideas*. She is the featured speaker on eight educational cheerleading videos: *Fundamentals of Basic Stunting, Creating Excitement With Transitional Stunting, Mastering Advanced Stunting, Physical Conditioning for Cheerleaders, Basic Jumping Technique, Cheerleading Chants, Pyramid Structure and Technique for Cheerleading,* and *Transitional Cheerleading Stunts*. She has traveled the United States, Canada, and Europe, speaking at conferences and clinics on numerous cheerleading topics about motivation, stunting technique, school spirit, and coaching.

Headridge began her love for cheerleading at Waterloo Junior High School in Maryland and continued to cheer throughout her high school and college years. She began coaching at Oak Harbor High School in Washington State in 1991. Her team, the Oak Harbor Wildcats, has won many state and national titles, including USA National High School Coed Champions. She is the founder of the Washington State Cheerleading Coaches Association.

Headridge and her husband, Bill, reside on picturesque Whidbey Island. They have two grown children, Misty and Stirling, and three grandchildren, Jamin, Mya, and Finn. She is enjoying her latest passion as a landscape photographer.

Robb Webb is originally from Morganton, North Carolina. He now resides in Lincolnton with his beautiful wife Jenna. He has served in the United States Navy and worked in the public school system as a language facilitator.

Webb has been involved with cheerleading for 23 years. As a former gym owner, he has trained several nationally ranked teams. He has had the opportunity to speak at conferences across the country on the topics of stunting, jumping, tumbling, and much more. He currently travels the United States, providing specialized stunt training to all levels, scholastic and all-stars. His motto: "Today's athletes are tomorrow's leaders. It is our responsibility as coaches to ensure we provide the tools and resources necessary to help young people become stronger adults."

He has been involved with several forms of art since childhood. His favorite mediums are pencil and pen and ink. Recently, he has begun working with watercolor and hopes to pursue a greater mastery of that wonderful art.